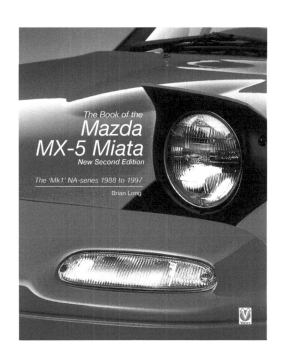

The Book of the
Mazda MX-5 Miata
New Second Edition

The 'Mk1' NA-series 1988 to 1997

Brian Long

T0386282

Other great books from Veloce –

RAC handbooks

Caring for your car – How to maintain & service your car (Fry)
Caring for your car's bodywork and interior (Nixon)
Efficient Driver's Handbook, The (Moss)
Electric Cars – The Future is Now! (Linde)
First aid for your car – Your expert guide to common problems & how to fix them (Collins)
How your car works (Linde)
Pass the MoT test! – How to check & prepare your car for the annual MoT test (Paxton)
Selling your car – How to make your car look great and how to sell it fast (Knight)
Simple fixes for your car – How to do small jobs for yourself and save money (Collins)

General

1½-litre GP Racing 1961-1965 (Whitelock)
AC Two-litre Saloons & Buckland Sportscars (Archibald)
Alfa Romeo 155/156/147 Competition Touring Cars (Collins)
Alfa Romeo Giulia Coupé GT & GTA (Tipler)
Alfa Romeo Montreal – The dream car that came true (Taylor)
Alfa Romeo Montreal – The Essential Companion (Taylor)
Alfa Tipo 33 (McDonough & Collins)
Alpine & Renault – The Development of the Revolutionary Turbo F1 Car 1968 to 1979 (Smith)
Alpine & Renault – The Sports Prototypes 1963 to 1969 (Smith)
Alpine & Renault – The Sports Prototypes 1973 to 1978 (Smith)
Anatomy of the Works Minis (Moylan)
Armstrong-Siddeley (Smith)
Art Deco and British Car Design (Down)
Automotive A-Z, Lane's Dictionary of Automotive Terms (Lane)
Automotive Mascots (Kay & Springate)
Bahamas Speed Weeks, The (O'Neil)
Bentley Continental, Corniche and Azure (Bennett)
Bentley MkVI, Rolls-Royce Silver Wraith, Dawn & Cloud/Bentley R & S-Series (Nutland)
Bluebird CN7 (Stevens)
BMC Competitions Department Secrets (Turner, Chambers & Browning)
BMW 5-Series (Cranswick)
BMW Z-Cars (Taylor)
BMW – The Power of M (Vivian)
British at Indianapolis, The (Wagstaff)
British Cars, The Complete Catalogue of, 1895-1975 (Culshaw & Horrobin)
BRM – A Mechanic's Tale (Salmon)
BRM V16 (Ludvigsen)
Bugatti Type 40 (Price)
Bugatti 46/50 Updated Edition (Price & Arbey)
Bugatti T44 & T49 (Price & Arbey)
Bugatti 57 2nd Edition (Price)
Carrera Panamericana, La (Tipler)
Chrysler 300 – America's Most Powerful Car 2nd Edition (Ackerson)
Chrysler PT Cruiser (Ackerson)
Citroën DS (Bobbitt)
Classic British Car Electrical Systems (Astley)
Cobra – The Real Thing! (Legate)
Concept Cars, How to illustrate and design (Dewey)
Cortina – Ford's Bestseller (Robson)
Coventry Climax Racing Engines (Hammill)
Daimler SP250 New Edition (Long)
Datsun Fairlady Roadster to 280ZX – The Z-Car Story (Long)
Dino – The V6 Ferrari (Long)
Dodge Challenger & Plymouth Barracuda (Grist)
Dodge Charger – Enduring Thunder (Ackerson)
Dodge Dynamite! (Grist)
Draw & Paint Cars – How to (Gardiner)
Drive on the Wild Side, A – 20 Extreme Driving Adventures From Around the World (Weaver)
Ferrari 288 GTO, The Book of the (Sackey)
Fiat & Abarth 124 Spider & Coupé (Tipler)
Fiat & Abarth 500 & 600 – 2nd Edition (Bobbitt)
Fiats, Great Small (Ward)
Fine Art of the Motorcycle Engine, The (Peirce)
Ford Cleveland 335-Series V8 engine 1970 to 1982 – The Essential Source Book (Hammill)

Ford F100/F150 Pick-up 1948-1996 (Ackerson)
Ford F150 Pick-up 1997-2005 (Ackerson)
Ford GT – Then, and Now (Streather)
Ford GT40 (Legate)
Ford Model Y (Roberts)
Ford Thunderbird From 1954, The Book of the (Long)
Formula 5000 Motor Racing, Back then ... and back now (Lawson)
Forza Minardi! (Vigar)
France: the essential guide for car enthusiasts – 200 things for the car enthusiast to see and do (Parish)
Grand Prix Ferrari – The Years of Enzo Ferrari's Power, 1948-1980 (Pritchard)
Grand Prix Ford – DFV-powered Formula 1 Cars (Robson)
GT – The World's Best GT Cars 1953-73 (Dawson)
Hillclimbing & Sprinting – The Essential Manual (Short & Wilkinson)
Honda NSX (Long)
Intermeccanica – The Story of the Prancing Bull (McCredie & Reisner)
Jaguar, The Rise of (Price)
Jaguar XJ 220 – The Inside Story (Moreton)
Jaguar XJ-S, The Book of the (Long)
Jeep CJ (Ackerson)
Jeep Wrangler (Ackerson)
Karmann-Ghia Coupé & Convertible (Bobbitt)
Kris Meeke – Intercontinental Rally Challenge Champion (McBride)
Lamborghini Miura Bible, The (Sackey)
Lamborghini Urraco, The Book of the (Landsem)
Lambretta Bible, The (Davies)
Lancia 037 (Collins)
Lancia Delta HF Integrale (Blaettel & Wagner)
Land Rover Series III Reborn (Porter)
Land Rover, The Half-ton Military (Cook)
Lea-Francis Story, The (Price)
Le Mans Panoramic (Ireland)
Lexus Story, The (Long)
Little book of microcars, the (Quellin)
Little book of smart, the – New Edition (Jackson)
Lola – The Illustrated History (1957-1977) (Starkey)
Lola – All the Sports Racing & Single-seater Racing Cars 1978-1997 (Starkey)
Lola T70 – The Racing History & Individual Chassis Record – 4th Edition (Starkey)
Lotus 49 (Oliver)
Marketingmobiles, The Wonderful Wacky World of (Hale)
Maserati 250F In Focus (Pritchard)
Mazda MX-5/Miata 1.6 Enthusiast's Workshop Manual (Grainger & Shoemark)
Mazda MX-5/Miata 1.8 Enthusiast's Workshop Manual (Grainger & Shoemark)
Mazda MX-5 Miata: The Book of the World's Favourite Sportscar (Long)
Mazda MX-5 Miata Roadster (Long)
Maximum Mini (Booij)
Mercedes-Benz SL – W113-series 1963-1971 (Long)
Mercedes-Benz SL & SLC – 107-series 1971-1989 (Long)
Mercedes-Benz SLK – R170 series 1996-2004 (Long)
MGA (Price Williams)
MGB & MGB GT– Expert Guide (Auto-doc Series) (Williams)
MGB Electrical Systems Updated & Revised Edition (Astley)
Micro Trucks (Mort)
Microcars at Large! (Quellin)
Mini Cooper – The Real Thing! (Tipler)
Mini Minor to Asia Minor (West)
Mitsubishi Lancer Evo, The Road Car & WRC Story (Long)
Monthléry, The Story of the Paris Autodrome (Boddy)
Morgan Maverick (Lawrence)
Morris Minor, 60 Years on the Road (Newell)
Motor Movies – The Posters! (Veysey)
Motor Racing – Reflections of a Lost Era (Carter)
Motor Racing – The Pursuit of Victory 1930-1962 (Carter)
Motor Racing – The Pursuit of Victory 1963-1972 (Wyatt/Sears)
Motor Racing Heroes – The Stories of 100 Greats (Newman)
Motorsport In colour, 1950s (Wainwright)
MV Agusta Fours, The book of the classic (Falloon)
Nissan 300ZX & 350Z – The Z-Car Story (Long)
Nissan GT-R Supercar: Born to race (Gorodji)
Northeast American Sports Car Races 1950-1959 (O'Neil)

Nothing Runs – Misadventures in the Classic, Collectable & Exotic Car Biz (Slutsky)
Pass the Theory and Practical Driving Tests (Gibson & Hoole)
Peking to Paris 2007 (Young)
Pontiac Firebird (Cranswick)
Porsche Boxster (Long)
Porsche 356 (2nd Edition) (Long)
Porsche 908 (Födisch, Neßhöver, Roßbach, Schwarz & Roßbach)
Porsche 911 Carrera – The Last of the Evolution (Corlett)
Porsche 911, The Book of the (Long)
Porsche 911R, RS & RSR, 4th Edition (Starkey)
Porsche 911SC 'Super Carrera' – The Essential Companion (Streather)
Porsche 914 & 914-6: The Definitive History of the Road & Competition Cars (Long)
Porsche 924 (Long)
The Porsche 924 Carreras - evolution to excellence (Smith)
Porsche 928 (Long)
Porsche 944 (Long)
Porsche 964, 993 & 996 Data Plate Code Breaker (Streather)
Porsche 993 'King Of Porsche' – The Essential Companion (Streather)
Porsche 996 'Supreme Porsche' – The Essential Companion (Streather)
Porsche Racing Cars – 1953 to 1975 (Long)
Porsche Racing Cars – 1976 to 2005 (Long)
Porsche – The Rally Story (Meredith)
Porsche: Three Generations of Genius (Meredith)
Preston Tucker & Others (Linde)
RAC Rally Action! (Gardiner)
RACING COLOURS – MOTOR RACING COMPOSITIONS 1908-2009 (Newman)
Rallye Sport Fords: The Inside Story (Moreton)
Roads with a View – England's greatest views and how to find them by road (Corfield)
Rolls-Royce Silver Shadow/Bentley T Series Corniche & Camargue – Revised & Enlarged Edition (Bobbitt)
Rolls-Royce Silver Spirit, Silver Spur & Bentley Mulsanne 2nd Edition (Bobbitt)
Runways & Racers (O'Neil)
Russian Motor Vehicles – Soviet Limousines 1930-2003 (Kelly)
Russian Motor Vehicles – The Czarist Period 1784 to 1917 (Kelly)
RX-7 – Mazda's Rotary Engine Sportscar (Updated & Revised New Edition) (Long)
Singer Story: Cars, Commercial Vehicles, Bicycles & Motorcycle (Atkinson)
Sleeping Beauties USA – abandoned classic cars & trucks (Marek)
SM – Citroën's Maserati-engined Supercar (Long & Claverol)
Speedway – Auto racing's ghost tracks (Collins & Ireland)
Sprite Caravans, The Story of (Jenkinson)
Standard Motor Company, The Book of the
Subaru Impreza: The Road Car And WRC Story (Long)
Supercar, How to Build your own (Thompson)
Tales from the Toolbox (Oliver)
Taxi! The Story of the 'London' Taxicab (Bobbitt)
Toleman Story, The (Hilton)
Toyota Celica & Supra, The Book of Toyota's Sports Coupés (Long)
Toyota MR2 Coupés & Spyders (Long)
Triumph TR6 (Kimberley)
TWR Story, The – Group A (Hughes & Scott)
Unraced (Collins)
Volkswagen Bus Book, The (Bobbitt)
Volkswagen Bus or Van to Camper, How to Convert (Porter)
Volkswagens of the World (Glen)
VW Beetle Cabriolet – The full story of the convertible Beetle (Bobbitt)
VW Beetle – The Car of the 20th Century (Copping)
VW Bus – 40 Years of Splitties, Bays & Wedges (Copping)
VW Bus Book, The (Bobbitt)
VW Golf: Five Generations of Fun (Copping & Cservenka)
VW – The Air-cooled Era (Copping)
VW T5 Camper Conversion Manual (Porter)
Which Oil? – Choosing the right oils & greases for your antique, vintage, veteran, classic or collector car (Michell)
Works Minis, The Last (Purves & Brenchley)
Works Rally Mechanic (Moylan)

www.veloce.co.uk

First published in April 2015, this revised paperback edition published October 2021 by Veloce Publishing Limited, Veloce House, Parkway Farm Business Park, Middle Farm Way, Poundbury, Dorchester DT1 3AR, England. Fax 01305 268864 / e-mail info@veloce.co.uk / web www.veloce.co.uk or www.velocebooks.com.
ISBN 978-1-787117-77-8. UPC 6-36847-01777-4

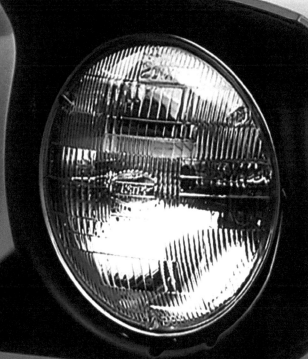

The Book of the
Mazda
MX-5 Miata
New Second Edition

The 'Mk1' NA-series 1988 to 1997

Brian Long

VELOCE

CONTENTS

INTRODUCTION & ACKNOWLEDGEMENTS

Introduction

Although I'd always had a soft spot for the first of the rotary-engined RX-7s, promoted so ably through the competition exploits of Tom Walkinshaw and Win Percy in the UK, and a whole host of racing drivers in the States, it wasn't until 1991 that I really sat up and took notice of the Mazda marque. That was the year I'd travelled to Le Mans with Simon Pickford, a great friend of mine, only to be disappointed that my beloved Jaguars had been beaten, but filled with respect for the green and orange machine that kept bombing away, keeping me awake most of the night with its glorious – if rather noisy – exhaust note.

By that time, of course, the Mazda MX-5 had taken the world by storm. Following its launch in 1989, journalists from all corners of the world simply ran out of superlatives – nothing on the sporting front had created such a strong impression since the first appearance of the Datsun 240Z. The Hiroshima concern had introduced its inexpensive convertible at just the right time, providing owners with all the fun of older machines without any of the hassle. As many contemporary commentators stated, Mazda had reinvented the sports car.

Before long, the MX-5 (also known as the Miata or Eunos Roadster depending on the market) had gained a reputation that was the envy of the motor industry. The team behind the two-seater was not prepared to rest on its laurels, though, and brought out special versions and a whole series of stunning prototypes. By the end of 1997,

the best part of 450,000 examples had been built, and a mini-industry for aftermarket parts had grown up around the vehicle in virtually every country it was sold.

Smitten by the MX-5 himself, Rod Grainger of Veloce asked me if I'd do a book on the history of the car. I must say I had my doubts at the time. With a 1968 Alfa Romeo Spider Veloce sitting in the garage, the little Mazda had always seemed too contrived, and all too clinical to me. Anyway, I took the project on in the autumn of 1997, hoping in the back of my mind that if I did the MX-5 book first, maybe Rod would ask me to do a volume on the RX-7 later.

As it happens, my neutral attitude towards the project doubtless helped, for I was able to see the real enthusiasm behind the concept and how incredibly thorough Mazda

had been, without falling into the trap of getting carried away by the myth and hysteria that seems to surround all cult cars, in much the same manner as rock and film stars. However, even from my standpoint, I didn't find many shortcomings, and grew to have a great deal of respect for the vehicle and the people behind it. After a few months of solid research, it was easy to see why the MX-5 had gained hoards of fans all over the world.

Meanwhile, between 1998 and 2006, *Mazda MX-5 Miata: The Book Of The World's Favourite Sportscar,* went to three editions with Veloce, each larger than its immediate predecessor due to the rapid evolution of the little two-seater, and I also became involved in a couple of other MX-5 titles in Japan along the way, too. For several years on and off, Rod and I have been trying to figure out how to go about keeping the Veloce book in print, as all the remaining copies were sold some time ago.

Unfortunately, for us to update the original Veloce title once more, it would make it not only very heavy and expensive, but it would also mean keeping some of the rare, attractive pictures from the early years quite small. We had no option as things were, trying to fit in the development story and production history of three distinctive vehicles into a reasonably sized and priced package. By splitting each generation into a separate volume, we can now do the illustrations justice, as well as add a few extra snippets of information along the way, as space is no longer an overwhelming concern.

We can hopefully do the NB and NC books in the near future, as they each have a strong following of their own, but what we have here is hopefully the definitive history of the First Generation MX-5 Miata – the NA series. Now is as good a time as any to note that the NA is also known as the 'M1' series in the States, but I will try and avoid this moniker as much as possible, as the NB became the 'M2', and that gets really confusing due to the same designation being used on a run of official NA-based specials built in Japan during the early 1990s. Ultimately, regardless of what you want to call the First Generation car, I hope you will enjoy the book…

Acknowledgements

Reading through the original list of acknowledgements brought back a lot of memories. My wife, Miho, was the first person mentioned, which is only right given the amount of effort she put in translating Japanese documents for days on end. Her input really helped put things in perspective, although it's fair to say she's happier watching me translating German documents nowadays, as my recent workload has increasingly taken me back towards European cars.

In Japan, the first chap that came to my aid was Tamotsu Maeda, who was stationed in the PR department at the time, although he was very much a hands-on engineer in his day. I met him at the Tokyo Show the other day, and I'm pleased to report that he's still the same larger than life character he always was. Kensaku Terasaki was also involved, along with the lovely Mayumi Handa, who had a barrage of faxes from me back then, but never complained, and co-ordinated interviews with various development team members, including one with Shunji Tanaka, who went to Kawasaki soon after. Ryota Ogawa took over from Han-chan, helping me no end with the RX-7 book that I did manage to do after all, and Kenichi Sagara came to my aid on many occasions before his services were snapped up by Volvo. The lady looking after me nowadays is Naoko Fujisaki, who works from Mazda's Tokyo office.

Special mention should be made of a few others, too. Takaharu Kobayakawa is an extraordinary man, and it is with great pride that I'm able to call him a friend. His weight opened a lot of doors at Mazda, for which I'm extremely grateful. Ironically, as the boss of that 1991 Le Mans campaign, after he retired from a lifelong career at Mazda, we went on to do the dealer training programme for Jaguar Japan together! As well as giving me a helping hand, Tom Matano wrote me a very special letter after the first book was published. It is something I shall treasure. Takao Kijima was also quick to react to my efforts, and it was wonderful to be able to include a Foreword by this engineering genius in the original titles. Although he has become a university lecturer now, I'm happy to say we've managed to stay in touch. Masanori Mizuochi was also very kind, filling in gaps on the M2 story, along with Hirotaka Tachibana, who has taken up a career in journalism after retiring from Mazda. I was also very lucky to have Shigenori Fukuda go over the text in his spare time, confirming and correcting statements with a level of enthusiasm displayed by all these legendary figures in MX-5 lore.

In America, Brian Betz, Ellen Clark, Jim Bright and Jennifer Newton came to the rescue, while Takahiro Tokura of Mazdaspeed, the folks at Mazda UK, and Bill Livingstone and Alan Beasley of IAD also pitched in. There were also a ton of tuning companies and aftermarket suppliers that provided material, adding some breath to the subject matter. Behind the scenes, too, people like Kenichi Kobayashi of Miki Press, Kenji Kikuchi of Nigensha, Michitake Isobe and Sachiko 'Miko' Miyoshi helped out in Japan, while Peter Hunter, Ian Robertson of Coventry Mazda and Paul Grogan of the MX-5 Owners Club did their bit, providing and checking historical material for me. Finally, the back cover features the work of another old friend – the late, great Yoshihiro Inomoto. His superb drawing of the NA1 model shows why he was known throughout the world as 'The Cutaway King'…

Brian Long
Chiba, Japan

Chapter 1

THE MAZDA STORY

The history of the Japanese motor industry is a complex one, moulded and shaped by government decisions taken in the early 1930s and the reconstruction of Japan following the Second World War.

Mazda's origins date back to January 1920, with the founding of the Toyo Cork Kogyo Company Ltd by Jujiro Matsuda. As the name suggests, the Hiroshima-based firm initially concerned itself with cork products, but in the following year, Matsuda decided to move into the manufacture of machinery.

Matsuda was born in August 1875, and, despite being brought up in the fishing trade, developed an early interest in metalworking. By the age of 19 he had his own business; sadly, destined to fail. After various other enterprises, Matsuda eventually decided to move into the supply of cork, as the First World War stopped exports from Europe and left Japan in short supply. When Europe started exporting again, Matsuda guided the company back into light industry.

The car was still not a popular means of transport for the Japanese at that time. In the early 1920s, there were still fewer than 15,000 vehicles in the country, so automobile production was not considered commercially viable. However, a few two-wheeled machines were built following the devastating Kanto earthquake of 1923.

That year brought a flurry of imported trucks and buses from the United States to get the country mobile again. Most of Japan's population was centred around the Tokyo Bay (Kanto) area, and the earthquake had

Jujiro Matsuda – entrepreneur and founder of the Mazda marque.

totally destroyed thousands of buildings, and most of the communications in Tokyo and Yokohama. Matsuda's Hiroshima-based concern, on the other side of the country, was not affected, and did its best to ease transport problems by building small two-stroke motorcycles.

The first vehicle to bear the Mazda name was a three-wheeled truck. Commercials of this type were built throughout the 1930s.

Although the firm still dealt in cork (this section of the business wasn't sold off until 1944), light industry became increasingly important. In line with this gradual shift in emphasis, in July 1927, the business was renamed the Toyo Kogyo Co Ltd, which roughly translates as the Orient Industry Company.

The Mazda marque

Production of Toyo machine tools began in 1929, but, by 1930, thoughts were already turning toward motor vehicles. Design work was initiated on a three-wheeled truck (the 482cc Mazda DA), which entered production in October 1931.

As an aside, there is an interesting story behind the choice of the Mazda name. In Persian mythology, the 'lord of light and wisdom' was called Ahura Mazdah. The Mazdah title sounded good in almost any language and had an ideal meaning, with the added bonus that the founder's family name was Matsuda (in Japanese, it sounds very similar to Mazdah). Subsequently, the letter 'h' was dropped and the Mazda marque was born.

The DA was a great success, and, within a few months of starting production, Toyo Kogyo began exporting the three-wheeled Mazda to Manchuria, an area of China occupied by Japan. Toyo Kogyo continued to develop the three-wheeler, giving it a larger engine, and also started to manufacture gauge blocks and machine drills.

The company's capital increased no fewer than four times during 1934, and the factory – based in the Fuchu area of Hiroshima – was duly enlarged. However, military considerations soon led the government to pass the 1936 Motorcar Manufacturing Enterprise Law. Although only Nissan, Toyota and Isuzu complied with the new law at the time, it effectively ended the activities of foreign car companies, with both Ford and General Motors initially cutting back production and then closing their factories in Japan during 1937.

Toyo Kogyo was forced to make munitions for the Army, although a few three-wheelers continued to leave the factory, despite the Enterprise Law. By 1940, Mazda had built a small prototype coupé, but before it could be developed further, production switched completely to armaments in the build-up to the Pacific War.

After the attack on Pearl Harbour, America declared war on Japan, but no-one could have foreseen the dreadful events that would follow. On 6 August 1945, Hiroshima became a scene of complete devastation. A broadcast from Tokyo Radio stated: "Most of Hiroshima no longer exists. The impact of the bomb was so terrific that practically all living things, human and animal, were literally seared to

A rare contemporary colour photograph of the K360 three-wheeler, built shortly after the Second World War.

death by the tremendous heat and pressure engendered by the blast." The Toyo Kogyo factory, partially sheltered by a hill, was just far enough away from the centre of the blast to escape heavy damage. Sadly, though, the bomb dropped by *Enola Gay* claimed 78,000 lives and injured countless others. The end of the Second World War came later that month, but it was many years before some kind of normality was restored to the lives of those – on both sides – who suffered as a result of the conflict.

Post-war growth

Although the factory was being used as a makeshift hospital and 'town hall,' Toyo Kogyo managed to resume production of the Mazda three-wheelers at the end of 1945. Three years later, the company's capital had doubled, and up to 200 vehicles were being built each week. Larger commercials were announced in 1950, but it was another decade before the company moved into the passenger car business.

Various laws were passed to help the Japanese motor industry, and gradually it found its feet. Production rose steadily, new roads were built, and Tokyo streets began to fill with Japanese cars rather than ageing imported models. Steel and components were being produced in

Mazda's three-wheeler acquired a more substantial appearance with the arrival of the CT series in 1950 (this is the 1953 CTA). Three-wheelers continued well into the 1960s, the T2000 of 1962 vintage having a two-ton load-carrying capacity.

The first Mazda car was the R360 Coupé of mid-1960, powered by a tiny air-cooled V-twin. Over 20,000 examples were sold in the first year of production.

A beautiful publicity shot of the Mazda Carol 360 Deluxe.

Japan, as by now most of the factories had been returned to their previous owners by the Occupational Forces, thus lessening the need to buy from foreign countries.

Commercial vehicles continued to sustain the Hiroshima concern, but, in April 1960, the company introduced its first car – the R360 Coupé. It went on sale in May with an air-cooled, V-twin engine mounted at the rear; although the 356cc unit developed only 16bhp, the R360 could be bought with either a manual or automatic transmission and was capable of 56mph (90kph). It sold exceptionally well, with over 20,000 being built in the first year.

After the war, a number of Japanese manufacturers had taken the opportunity to enter into technical co-operation agreements with companies in the west. The Toyo Kogyo concern was quite late in taking up this offer, but eventually, in mid-1961, signed a deal with NSU of Germany.

NSU held the rights to the Wankel rotary engine, a rather advanced piece of engineering. It was felt that being the first vehicle builder in Japan to acquire this technology would enable Mazda to catch up with the likes of Nissan and Toyota, thus ensuring its survival.

Over the next five years, while the rotary engine was being developed, Toyo Kogyo introduced a number of new Mazda cars – the Carol P360 and P600, the first generation of Familia models, and the Luce 1500. (The coachwork on the latter was designed by a famous Italian styling house; in fact, Giugiaro has been credited with the design during his time with Bertone.)

Meanwhile, cumulative production of cars and commercials reached one million units in March 1963; two years later, the Miyoshi Proving Ground was completed. By this time, Toyo Kogyo was the third largest car producer in Japan, continually expanding operations at a staggering rate. In 1966, a new passenger car plant opened in Hiroshima, and, in the following year, full-scale exports for the European market began.

The rotary revolution
Toyo Kogyo – under the leadership of Jujiro Matsuda's son, Tsuneji, since 1951 – was certainly a forward-thinking organisation, installing its first computer system at Hiroshima as early as 1958. Six years later, at the 1964 Tokyo Show (held at Harumi that year), the Mazda Cosmo Sport 110S made its debut.

Powered by the company's first Wankel engine, it was extremely advanced, and gave the Rotary Engine Development Division more than a few teething problems in the early days. It underwent an extraordinary period of development before going on sale to the public, with a total of 60 pre-production models road tested. Consequently, the Mazda Cosmo did not go on sale until 30 May 1967, by which time the company's engineers had perfected the power unit. Selling at 1,580,000 yen, it was very costly (only the Toyota 2000GT was more expensive in the sports car sector of the Japanese market), and this was reflected in a total run, from 1967 to 1972, of just 1519 units.

In October 1969, the Japan Automatic Transmission Company (JATCO) was formed: a joint venture between Toyo Kogyo, Ford and Nissan for the manufacture of automatic gearboxes. The rotary engine passed Federal tests that year, and exports to the United States began shortly afterwards. The first cars – with both rotary and more conventional powerplants appearing in the line-up – arrived there in the spring of 1970. Within a year, Mazda dealerships were selling vehicles before there was even time to unload them from the transporters.

Following the death of Tsuneji Matsuda in November 1970 (he was 74), the reins were passed to his son, Kohei, the third generation of the Matsuda family to head

The rotary-engined Cosmo Sport 110S of 1967. Around 350 of these early models were built before the Cosmo underwent a minor face-life in mid-1968. Its high price tag limited total sales to just over 1500 units over a six-year production run.

the company. There was a whole string of important introductions during the early 1970s: the Mazda Capella (RX-2) was followed by the Savanna (RX-3) and, in 1972, the Luce (RX-4) made its debut. Mazda cars were now beginning to outsell trucks year after year. By the end of 1972, cumulative production had reached a staggering five million units, and the Mazda Technical Centre had been established in Irvine, California.

The oil crisis held up a number of interesting projects, such as the X020G 2+2 coupé. Rotary units, some rated up to 200bhp, were being prepared, but the timing, sadly, was all wrong, and sales of rotary-engined models as a whole began to suffer as fuel economy became an overriding consideration for new car buyers. As a result, Toyo Kogyo soon ran into financial troubles and had to turn to the Sumitomo Bank for help to keep the business

The elegant lines of the Luce Rotary Coupé – a pillarless, two-door model based on the Luce 1500 saloon.

The car you've waited 85 years for.

In 1885, the internal combustion engine was invented and the motor car as we know it was born. It didn't look much and the engine went-up-and-down-and-in-and-out-and-eventually-round-and-round.

Most car engines still work on this rather inefficient 19th century principle.

But now there's the Mazda R.100 Coupe.

As modern as men on the moon.

It has a revolutionary rotary engine* that produces 100 bhp, yet is only half the size and weight of a conventional engine. Twin rotors go round and round, smoothly, silently and without vibration.

The flow of force is never interrupted by reciprocating parts like pistons, valves and rods. The result is one of the most effortless drives imaginable – and all Mazda cars are designed to run on 2-star petrol.

To match the newer-than-new character of the R.100, Mazda have given it matchless looks and comfort. Racy fast-back styling and 'this car means business' black mesh grille with large rectangular headlights.

Inside, the R.100 goes on looking like a sports

car, sporting a wood-rimmed steering wheel, a nifty shifty gear lever, reclining front seats with headrests and full instrumentation which looks as good as it's good for looking at. To go with all that, it very sportingly seats four. Don't wait any longer. 85 years have been long enough. See the phenomenal Mazda R.100 right away.

Recommended retail price of the R.100 Coupe is £1,649.18.1 inc. p.t. Other Mazda models available in the U.K. are the 1800 Saloon (£1,189.13.11 inc. p.t.); the 1200 Saloon (£879.12.6 inc. p.t.) and the 1200 Estate (£949.9.6 inc. p.t.)

To: Industria (London) Ltd., 248 Holloway Rd., London N.7.
Please forward name of nearest dealer and full details of the new Mazda R.100.
Name
Address
Dept.MS

MAZDA

Toyo Kogyo Co., Ltd., Hiroshima, Japan
Sole U.K. Concessionaires: Industria (London) Ltd., 248 Holloway Road, N.7. Telephone: 01-607 8181 Telex: 23851

*Mazda rotary engine licensed by NSU/WANKEL

MOTOR SPORT, MARCH 1970 **177**

A British advertisement for the Mazda R100 Coupé dating from March 1970. Known in Japan as the Familia Rotary Coupé, it was also sold in the United States, but acquired round headlights for that market.

afloat. The company eventually received the bank's backing, but the Matsuda family lost some of its power in the process.

The RX-7 Savanna

1977 saw the introduction of the Familia (the original GLC/323, powered by a conventional four-stroke engine), which doubtless helped combat the downturn in Mazda sales. However, it was the car launched the following year that was significant to enthusiasts of sporting machinery.

Things were starting to happen in Japan as far as the sports car world was concerned. Nissan had been building the highly-successful Fairlady Z since late 1969, but, during 1978, it took a distinct move upmarket. Mazda had launched the RX-7 (known in Japan as the Savanna) in March 1978, and, in effect, this took the market position of the old Fairlady Z as a cheap but competent sports car, selling for 1,230,000 yen.

As Kohei Matsuda said in late-1977: "A two-seater sports car may well represent the ultimate design compliment for the rotary engine." He was absolutely right. The Mazda marque had already acquired a reputation

The home market Savanna GT of 1972, better known abroad as the RX-3. Like the RX-2 (which was also rotary-engined), it came as an attractive coupé (as seen here) or with four-door saloon bodywork. An estate version augmented the RX-3 range.

among motorsport enthusiasts for its sporting machines, but the rotary-engined RX-7 established the Japanese car maker all over the world, and signalled a turnaround in the fortunes of the Wankel power unit.

Of course, the RX-7 was admired on the home market as well, and duly received the 'Japanese Car of the Year' award. However, by the time it was officially put on sale, Yoshiki Yamasaki had become the head of the company – the first non-Matsuda family member to do so since 1922.

Revival, and links with Ford

Sales started to pick up again after the introduction of the conventionally powered Familia family car and the immensely popular RX-7. Cumulative production reached ten million vehicles in 1979, but, in November that year, Ford acquired a 24.5 per cent equity stake in Mazda. Within three years, Mazda was marketing Ford brand vehicles through its Autorama sales channel in Japan. This arrangement actually worked both ways, as a number of Mazdas (such as the B-series pick-up) had been badged

as Fords in the States, and vehicles were later developed jointly on both sides of the Pacific.

In the meantime, 1980 brought with it the introduction of the front-wheel drive Mazda Familia (also known as the GLC or 323 depending on the market). The Familia was presented with the coveted 1980-1981 'Japanese Car of the Year' award, and over one million had been produced by 1982.

As a matter of interest, Japanese manufacturers built seven million vehicles between them during 1980, helping Japan to become the world's number one car-producing country. Mazda (North America) Inc. – better-known as MANA – was established during 1981, and became a key organisation in the initial stages of the MX-5's development. Despite unfavourable exchange rates, almost 170,000 Mazdas were sold in the States that year, with the GLC being a bestseller in the economy sector, and the face-lifed RX-7 appealing to the enthusiasts.

1982 saw the introduction of the fwd Mazda Capella (or 626). It was immediately given the 1982-1983 'Japanese Car of the Year' award in its native country, but

Although not the most interesting Mazda ever built, the Familia (known as the GLC in America and the 323 elsewhere), with its conventional fuel efficient engine, helped Toyo Kogyo to survive an uncertain period in the company's history. This American advert dates from early 1978.

The Mazda RX-7, seen here in home market Limited form, was immensely popular in America, despite the fuel crisis and unfavourable exchange rates. An excellent competition record in the United States probably helped convince enthusiasts, and the car also received a number of awards in Japan.

The RX-7 was an instant hit in Britain. Tom Walkinshaw won his class in one in the BTCC in 1979, whilst Win Percy took the Championship outright with the RX-7 in 1980 and 1981. Walkinshaw had prepared Percy's car, and these are TWR-modified road cars from 1981. From left to right: the front-wheel drive 323, the 626 Coupé, and the RX-7 Turbo.

it also received a large number of prestigious accolades overseas, including being named *Motor Trend* magazine's 1983 'Import Car of the Year.' Sales in America continued to climb as the Mazda range attracted an ever wider audience.

Toyo Kogyo entered into an 8 per cent capital tie-up with Kia Motors in 1983, and cumulative production reached 15 million units. From a very small beginning, the Mazda marque had grown at great speed, and now had a range of vehicles that could compete in all markets, challenging established manufacturers throughout the world. However, Toyo Kogyo was not yet satisfied with its achievements ...

Chapter 2

BIRTH OF THE MAZDA ROADSTER

Kenichi Yamamoto, RJC 'Person of the Year' 1991-92, and a key figure in Mazda's automotive history.

The Toyo Kogyo business was renamed the Mazda Motor Corporation on 1 May 1984, with Kenichi Yamamoto elected President shortly after his 62nd birthday. Born in September 1922, the former MD had served Toyo Kogyo for many years, and had been the company's Chief Engineer since January 1978.

Yamamoto had seen a vast number of changes along the way in both technology (he had been responsible for designing a V-twin engine for the three-wheeled Mazda trucks shortly after the war, and was heavily involved with the R360 and its descendants; he was also one of the key people behind the development of the Mazda rotary engine), and in the growth of the company as a leading car manufacturer. However, behind all of Yamamoto's achievements in the field of engineering was an underlying enthusiasm for his work – an important factor which would have a bearing on the future.

MANA

Mazda (North America) Inc. (or MANA) had a Product Planning & Research (PP&R) arm, which was managed by Shigenori Fukuda. The idea behind this department was that its findings would give Mazda a much better feel for its market, so that future vehicles could be tailored specifically to suit the tastes of different countries.

One of the first Americans to join the PP&R office was Bob Hall, a true car enthusiast with a background in automotive journalism. Hall, having been brought up

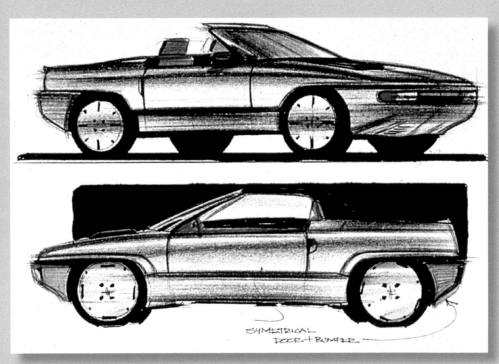

The MANA team actually drew a diverse range of sports car proposals, but, in reality, it was the lightweight open two-seater that appealed the most.

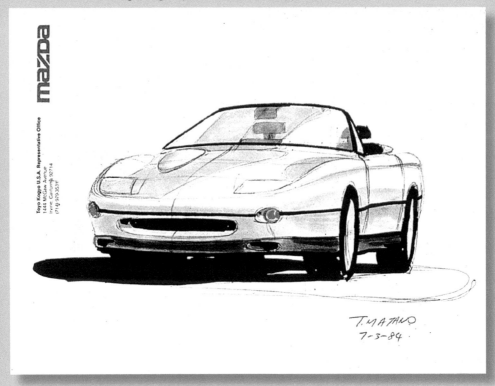

An original design sketch from Tom Matano, dated March 1984.

A roadster with a detachable hard-top in place. A closed coupé was also investigated, at least on paper.

Another of the design drawings submitted by MANA for its ideal lightweight sports car. According to Fukuda-san, hundreds of sketches were produced, a number of the proposals resembling vehicles like the Morgan three-wheeler, Lotus Seven, and the Porsche 550 Spyder.

around British sports cars, was keen on the idea of a modern equivalent. In fact, when casually asked at the end of a meeting with Kenichi Yamamoto in the spring of 1979 (when Hall was still working as a journalist), what he would like to see Toyo Kogyo building, he suggested that Mazda should make a lightweight sports car that would sell at a price even cheaper than the RX-7's.

On a trip to the 1983 Pebble Beach concours event, Hall soon found he was not alone in this idea. Fukuda, one of the group evaluating the RX-7 in the all-important American market, was asked by Hall what type of car he would like to design next. His reply was "a lightweight sports car." Naturally, this drew quite an eager response, and Hall's Japanese soon turned into excited English. Needless to say, by the end of the journey (after Hall had been stopped for speeding as his enthusiasm grew by the mile), Fukuda-san's English had improved no end!

Not long after this, an appraisal entitled *What is a Sports Car to an American?* was sent through to Head Office. This was quite a lengthy piece, but the most important paragraphs read as follows: "Sports cars must have a degree of performance, but more importantly, they must be fun to drive. A low-cost sports car doesn't need 0.81g lateral acceleration or 0-60 in 8.5 seconds. It has to, as one journalist succintly put it, 'feel faster than it is, but it doesn't have to be fast in absolute terms.' Of course, a sports car musn't be a sluggard either, so it is a classic example of searching for the happy medium.

"Appearance (particularly one's first impression) and performance are obvious things which make a sports car, but there are a couple of intangibles, too. Not the least of these is image. If you look back in history, all (not some or most, but all) of the successful sports cars have developed a cult-like following of enthusiasts, a core of people who have an almost maniacal enthusiasm for the particular make and model of car they own – MG or Lotus Elan enthusiasts, for example. Most of these people would never race or rally their car, but they won't buy anything else. This image is essential to a successful sports car. The MGs all had it – Saab's Sonnet never did. Any TR-series Triumph possessed this element, but try as hard as it could, Sunbeam wasn't ever able to develop such an image for the Alpine.

"There have also been a lot more successful convertible sports cars than coupés, at least in the United States and Canada. The Opel GT, Marcos 1800, Glas 1700 GT, Lancia Montecarlo (Scorpion in America), Simca 1000 and (in later forms) Saab Sonnet were all pretty, but there wasn't a convertible (or a success) among them. Even Targas are not open cars to most sports car owners. This is not to say that a light sports car cannot succeed without a convertible [top], but an $8000 convertible among a flock of $9000 –$12,000 coupés and Targas should be as popular as beer at a baseball stadium."

It was obvious that the people at MANA (known as MRA nowadays) thought America was in need of an affordable sports car. At this stage in the proceedings, however, nothing was heard from Hiroshima.

An LWS

A friend of the author, Yoshihiko Matsuo, Chief Designer of the original Fairlady Z (240Z) and now a design consultant, gave his definition of a modern sports car in a recent interview: "It must be a two-passenger automobile with attractive body styling designed for high speed, highly-responsive driving. The engine must have reserves of power even at high rpm. It should have a manual transmission with a good feel and a fully functional cockpit, and support pleasant high speed handling. To state it as a category, I would say that sports cars belong to a category somewhere between specialty cars and racing prototypes. Also, I believe, there are two main types of sports cars; one the Lightweight Sports Car and the other the Super Sports Car."

The Mazda RX-7 wasn't exactly lightweight, but it was nearer the lightweight concept than most. Weighing in at around 1100kg (2420lb), it was substantially lighter than Nissan's S130 series Fairlady (280ZX), and the recently introduced Z31 models. But the RX-7 was destined to follow the Fairlady in its move upmarket: the P747 would be bigger, faster, heavier, and better-equipped. In other words, the second generation RX-7 was going to be a Super Sports Car.

The first generation RX-7 sold in massive numbers in the States, just like the original affordable Japanese sports car of the Seventies, the 240Z. The Toyota Celica was another success story. Of course, exchange rates at the time helped, but these cars were not the pure flukes some would have you believe – nothing in Japanese business

happens by chance. By careful research, the Japanese had found the formula: offer excellent value-for-money in an attractive, reliable package, and it's a licence to print money.

However, with the new RX-7 scheduled for the 1986 model year (work had started on it in 1981), this was going to leave a void in the market as far as Japanese manufacturers were concerned. Toyota immediately spotted this niche and tried to fill it with the mid-engined MR2, but in America – the world's biggest sports car market – it was not as successful as was hoped, probably because Pontiac brought out the Fiero just beforehand. Honda also saw the gap and launched the sporty front-engined, front-wheel drive CRX, but this could never be considered a true sports car in the great tradition of the S500, S600 and S800 roadsters.

The Mazda marque was flying high in the States at that time, with the RX-7 dominating the IMSA racing scene and the SCCA Pro-Rally series. Kenichi Yamamoto knew that a true LWS – an abbreviation of lightweight sports car, a term used within the trade in much the same way as MPV (multi-purpose vehicle), and so on – would potentially have the market to itself and further strengthen Mazda's sporting image.

Yamamoto had got the sports car bug after Hirotaka Tachibana of the Experimental Department and Takaharu Kobayakawa (one of Yamamoto's most respected engineers who had been Chief Engineer on the RX-7 since 1986) – both LWS enthusiasts of the highest order – had encouraged him to take a business trip to Tokyo via the mountain roads around Hakone in a Triumph Spitfire. After this, he knew that Mazda should try and develop a similar vehicle. Judging by MANA's essay sent to Hiroshima in 1982, the staff there also thought the market needed an entry level sports car as well.

The Mazda Technical Research Centre in Hiroshima was still in the planning stage (it opened in 1985), so as something of a stop-gap, in November 1983, the company established a programme to allow its designers to think up and develop ideas for vehicles outside their recognised range. This programme was given the bizarre name, 'Off-Line, …Go, Go' – the latter part being taken to mean 55, as in projects having a 55 percent chance of success, thus keeping things sensible.

Michinori Yamanouchi, Mazda's Managing Director, hoped that this programme would encourage the engineering and design staff to take a fresh approach and, indeed Off-Line, Go, Go (or OGG) elicited some novel proposals. The subject of this book was one of the projects to be tackled off-line – a lightweight sports car.

A competition

Once the LWS project had been chosen, there was the matter of which layout to go for. It was decided that the three main possibilities – FR (front engine, rear-wheel drive), FF (front engine, front-wheel drive), and MR (mid-

engine, rear-wheel drive) – would be split so that each idea could be developed properly. After some far from subtle hints, the FR layout went to MANA in the States, while the FF and MR cars were assigned to the Tokyo Design Studio in Japan. The resulting designs would then go through two rounds of judging in Hiroshima and, ultimately, a winner declared. Masakatsu Kato, who was behind many of Mazda's concept cars, was given the task of overseeing the project, code number P729.

Although there were no firm plans for the LWS as yet, Mazda was seriously considering producing a Familia Cabriolet. Mark Jordan, who had joined MANA in January 1983, was put in charge of the project. The son of Chuck Jordan (the head of design at General Motors), he came from talented stock. A car was duly built, and the model eventually joined the Mazda line-up.

However, the team at MANA was far more interested in the LWS project. By this time, Fukuda, Jordan, and stylist Masao Yagi (Fukuda's assistant who had been sent to the States from Hiroshima), had already began working on their ideal open sports car. Tsutomu (Tom) Matano joined MANA at the end of 1983 as head of the design section, having previously worked for GM and BMW, earning an excellent reputation along the way.

Tom Matano wasn't particularly happy with the facilities at MANA when he first moved there (most of MANA's money at that time came from fitting air conditioning units bought in the States), although the LWS project that he took over had great appeal. "When I joined Mazda," he said, "the first project I worked on was the Miata, and I thought this was a good chance for me to really put my emotions and passions together to make a car."

August 1984. The first model from MANA which set the LWS project in motion. Tom Matano said his team had set out "to recapture the spirit of the British sports car," but no-one could have anticipated at the time the huge success of the subsequent production model.

The Tokyo Design Studio's FF coupé in profile. The drawings based around this layout were perhaps better than the full-sized clay, although the nose was very attractive. A convertible had also been suggested in the early stages of the design process.

The MR design submitted by Sato and Suzuki. An interesting proposal, the overall dimensions were very close to those of the recently introduced Toyota MR2.

Front three-quarter shot of the MR proposal.

Having said that it was the Bertone-styled Alfa Romeo Giulia Canguro of 1964 which inspired him to become a car designer in the first place, Matano's view concerning the background to the project was quite significant: "I think what we're looking for is the simplicity of the era, say, the Sixties. We want to get back to a relationship between car and driver that simply brings fun [to the owner]. At a time when the British sports cars had all gone ... due to either safety rules or emission rules and so forth, the fun element was really disappearing out of the market. And again, another urge was to provide the type of car that we loved when we were younger ... [We thought] a small sports car with a convertible [top] has to have a place in the future as it had in the past."

Shortly after Matano joined the team, a layout engineer by the name of Norman Garrett III signed up for MANA as well. Given that the American LWS would use an

A rear view of the MR model. In fact, the MR layout was always going to struggle, as Masaaki Watanabe had built an experimental mid-engined 323 and dismissed it on NVH (Noise, Vibration and Harshness) grounds.

MANA's Duo 101 in profile.

A front view of the FR model. Note the pop-up headlights, the stylish air intake and small door mirrors.

The attractive Kamm tail of the Duo 101. Neat touches abound, such as the hidden door releases and fairing on the rear deck.

FR layout (the one preferred by most traditional sports car enthusiasts and the MANA team itself), Garrett decided to use components from the existing range – an old rwd GLC (323) engine and transmission, and MacPherson struts all-round for the suspension.

Although a fresh approach could have been used (that was the reason behind the formation of OGG, after all), it was hoped that by using parts that could be easily sourced from within the organisation, the project stood more chance of being accepted.

Meanwhile, two lightweight coupés were being designed in the Tokyo Design Studio; one, a front-wheel drive model (FF), and the other, a mid-engined (MR) vehicle. The FF design had a distinct advantage, as the 323 was moving in this direction and would make an obvious donor car if the design was allowed to progress.

The success of the Honda CRX also helped promote this configuration.

Having been involved with the RX-7, Yoichi Sato was quite keen to produce a car to compete with the CRX, and set about his task with the help of Hideki Suzuki in their small office in the Gotanda district of Tokyo, not far from Haneda Airport. Early drawings included a convertible but, eventually, an attractive coupé was settled on. However, the mid-engined vehicle, with its wedge shape and sharp roofline, was more distinctive. Indeed, when the competitors met for the first round of the contest in April 1984, it was the MR machine that looked the most impressive on paper.

The MANA proposal was not totally without support, though, as Toriyama-san (Mazda's export man and MANA President) was quite enthusiastic about the open car.

The Duo 101 with its hard-top in place. Shigenori Fukuda can be seen in the middle of this picture, his jacket draped over his shoulder.

Seconds out, Round Two ...

When the second round of competition was held in August, the FF design was looking odds-on favourite. The MR design, meanwhile, had an uphill struggle on its hands. In reality, it was almost doomed from the start, as Masaaki Watanabe had already built a Familia with the MR layout and declared it unsuitable for production. Extra bulkheads would have insulated the noise and heat build-up, but, naturally, weight then increases as a result. It had dimensions very close to those of the recently announced Toyota MR2, and with the Pontiac Fiero also available, the mid-engined sports car market was probably better catered for than it had been since the 1970s.

The second phase of the competition was to present full-scale clays, and, through this process, the MANA proposal suddenly came alive. Even Sato was impressed, saying: "Their full-size model was a quantum leap from those flat sketches."

The design (which was actually the first clay to be built at the Irvine studio) was christened the 'Duo 101' by the staff at MANA – Duo apparently signifying that either a hard-top or soft-top could be used.

Fukuda and Hall put forward a whole host of reasons outlining why the FR layout was more suitable in a car of this type, and even put together a video presentation to try and sway the judges' decision. It was a very professional approach which ultimately paid off. The MANA team won and was therefore destined to play an important part in the early stages of Mazda's LWS project.

A brave decision?

The decision to go for the convertible may have seemed a brave move, but, in retrospect, there was an obvious hole in the market. The Alfa Romeo Spider was suffering from a lack of investment and ongoing development, and the Fiat Spider, latterly badged as a Pininfarina model, was about to fade away.

There wasn't really much else available, unless one was willing to look at low-volume models, special conversions on existing coupés, or very expensive convertibles. But it wasn't always this way: look in any American monthly magazine from the 1960s and there will almost certainly be more adverts for open British sports cars than for any homegrown products. However, by 1970, British manufacturers had completely lost their stronghold on the American market.

Forthcoming Federal regulations seemed to signal the end of the convertible, but it's much too easy to cite this as the sole reason for the extinction of the cheap sporty models eminating from UK shores. In fact, a number of factors contributed, with the car builders having to take at least some of the blame for poor build quality, archaic specifications, and a distinct lack of customer care.

Reliability problems were another factor. The author has owned a string of cars which would appeal to the enthusiast, so can confirm as well as anyone that the occasional problem is accepted and passed off as thoroughbred temperament. However, after a while it soon becomes wearing, and, with the introduction of the

The completed IAD running prototype, built in glassfibre and featuring a backbone chassis. It was based on the first MANA clay – the second clay had the air intake removed at the front, relocated door handles, and different rear lights.

A rear view of the V705. Note the exceptionally large rear screen area and the Toyota reference on the number plate – typical British humour.

Datsun Fairlady roadsters (and then the legendary 240Z), many sports car enthusiasts were converted to Japanese products which not only spent more time on the road instead of in the garage, but also offered exceptional value for money.

This spoilt the Americans, who witnessed the qualities of Japanese cars in SCCA racing as well. When the Triumph TR7 eventually became available as a convertible (it was designed as a pure coupé from the start as it was thought soft-top cars would be banned in the US), an American magazine carried out a loyalty survey to see if existing owners would buy another. In stark contrast to cars like the 240Z and RX-7, the results were some of the worst recorded. In Europe, too, although sports car buyers were a little less receptive to these Oriental impersonators, the Japanese were certainly making inroads.

Japan had not built many convertibles since the war, and most of them from the early 1980s were coupés converted to cabriolets by third parties. Avatar did this with the first generation RX-7 before Mazda produced its own convertible on the second generation RX-7. Other notable examples included ASC's work on the Celica, and Richard Straman's 300ZX and cheap little roadster based on the Honda Civic. Interestingly, all of these conversions were carried out in North America.

Looking further back in history, the Datsun DC-3 was probably the first purpose-built Japanese convertible, sold during 1952. Nissan built a few soft-top prototypes before launching the Datsun Fairlady Roadsters. There was also a prototype 240Z drophead, which, sadly, failed to make it into production due to proposed Federal regulations threatening to stamp out open cars. There was also the Mikasa, but very few were sold. Other rarities included the Prince Skyline Sport Convertible and Daihatsu Compagno. Honda built a run of successful roadsters, and Toyota took the roof off a 2000GT for a James Bond movie, but it wasn't until the third generation Celica that Toyota listed a convertible in its line-up. The examples mentioned here show that the Japanese had hardly flooded the market with convertibles, the best-selling models having gone out of production in the late 1960s.

Ultimately, the American authorities didn't pass the regulations outlawing the soft-top, but even though the convertible's future seemed assured, surprisingly few manufacturers took the opportunity to build one. The consensus of opinion seemed to be that the convertible market had simply ceased to exist after 1970. Maybe Mazda was right to explore the possibilities, and, by using the OGG route, the company didn't have to commit itself

When the IAD-built V705 prototype arrived in America for its Santa Barbara excursion, the RX-7 wheels were changed for some multi-spoke items that would not give a clue to the car's true identity. Arriving on the back of a car transporter wrapped in a grey cover, the vehicle was made ready for its drive around the local area, but its number plates from a Mazda distributor soon gave the game away.

fully until totally satisfied there was still sufficient interest. Although the LWS project was not guaranteed production status at this stage, the team at MANA was convinced it would eventually find its way into the showrooms.

IAD
In September 1984, International Automotive Design, better-known as IAD, was asked by Mazda to become involved with the LWS project. Based in Worthing in the south of England, IAD was founded by the late John Shute (an ex-GM body engineer and avid collector of MGs) in the early 1970s. Shute was familiar to the trade, and IAD soon gained an excellent reputation for developing prototypes.

Mazda wanted its new car to have a British flavour and actually commissioned IAD not only to build a running prototype based on the Duo 101, but also to carry out evaluations on a number of British classics. Cars – including the first Lotus Elan – were tested at the MIRA facility in the centre of England and reports compiled.

A fibreglass lookalike open body and makeshift interior were constructed around mechanical components from a selection of Mazda models: the 1.4-litre engine and transmission came from a rwd Familia, the front suspension and wheels were taken from an early RX-7, and the rear suspension was from a Luce (929). The interesting part of the prototype was the use of a backbone chassis, designed and built in-house by IAD.

Given the code number V705 by Mazda, the car – with its fibreglass body (a feature Kato had insisted on at this early stage), backbone chassis and FR layout –

was, in effect, the Japanese equivalent of the original Lotus Elan. The V705 was fully-functional and, under the direction of Project Manager, Bill Livingstone, it was eventually completed in August 1985.

California dreamin'
The enthusiastic team at MANA had done little on the LWS project since it was handed over to IAD, but work had recently started again to enable some subtle design changes to the body, the eventual result being the S-2 clay. In the meantime, on 17 September 1985, Mazda staff from Japan and America met up in Worthing to view and drive the IAD prototype in England.

On the first day, the car was viewed in the IAD works, but on the second day the group, led by Masakatsu Kato, was taken to the Ministry of Defence test track not too far from IAD, where the V705 was compared on a high speed loop, a road course and a skidpan with a Fiat X1/9, a Toyota MR2, and the new Reliant Scimitar. Everyone was exceptionally happy with the vehicle. Mark Jordan wrote in his report that IAD "did an excellent job. After testing the car, it felt very pleasing ..."

The car was then scheduled to be shipped back to Japan, but, on the orders of Managing Director, Masataka Matsui, newly-appointed head of the Technical Research Centre, it was sent to the States instead. Matsui wanted to see the new machine in its natural environment, which made sense, but it was also very risky as the car could have been spotted by someone from the motoring journals. For this reason, somewhere that wasn't too busy

Toshihiko Hirai, the MX-5's Chief Engineer, pictured by the author during a trip to Hiroshima. Following a spell as a university lecturer, he was recently inducted into JAHFA.

had to be chosen. After much deliberation, Santa Barbara seemed the ideal place.

In mid-October, Matsui arrived in California to see the new car in the setting it was designed for. MANA had assembled a small group of cars for comparison (an RX-7, a Triumph Spitfire, and a Honda convertible by the Straman concern), and took the V705 to Santa Barbara on a car transporter. Anyone remotely interested in cars immediately came to look at the new vehicle, which wasn't exactly anonymous as it carried Californian plates borrowed from a local distributor.

Unfortunately, whilst out driving, the Mazda crew came across a number of journalists testing cars, and the registration plates quickly gave the game away. Bob Hall, being an ex-writer, explained the situation and somehow managed to get the motoring scribes to agree not to publish any photographs.

In retrospect, Fukuda thought it was a mistake to expose the car so

early. Overall, though, it was a highly successful day. Matsui was more than happy with the public response at this impromptu clinic. At dinner with the MANA team that evening, Matsui was convinced that the LWS had potential and declared "I think we should build this car." More importantly, when he returned to Hiroshima, he gave the LWS project his full recommendation.

Virtual reality

1985 saw the introduction of the all-new fwd Mazda Familia (323) series in Japan, and the second generation Savanna RX-7. The RX-7 was duly named 1986 'Import Car of the Year' by *Motor Trend* magazine.

A number of interesting concept cars appeared as well. Suzuki displayed its R/S1 LWS at the 1985 Tokyo Show. However, somewhat surprisingly, despite favourable reactions, the vehicle never made it into production, so the way was still clear for Mazda. The Hiroshima marque displayed the MX-03, a four-wheel drive, four-wheel steer coupé designed by Kato, at the same event. With 2+2 seating, it was sportier than the MX-02 from two years earlier (which was quite staid by comparison), but was destined to remain a prototype.

Shigenori Fukuda returned to Japan to take up the post of General Manager of the Design Division. Having been closely involved with the LWS project from its birth, Fukuda was obviously keen to see it through to the end, as it was the epitome of his 'Romantic Engineering' concept. However, the LWS was still not guaranteed a place in the Mazda line-up. At the end of the 1980s, Fukuda stated that "the project was interrupted several times." In fact, Shunji Tanaka feels that had Fukuda not returned to Japan, the LWS might never have seen the light of day.

There were a number of reasons for having doubts about the LWS's future. Mazda had already approved its new MPV which, with the benefit of hindsight, was

The third and final clay produced by MANA. The front indicators were a little too large, and the shape of the air intake and tail graphics were further refined in Japan.

An interview with Shunji Tanaka (Chief Designer on the M1 body)

Mr Tanaka: "Today, there are many open two-seater cars on the market. However, in 1986, there was nothing resembling the open two-seater concept available, and it was hard even to carry out market research effectively. I remember that at the time we really struggled to get this car into production."

Miho Long: *"Could you tell us which are your favourite parts of the design, and why?"*

Mr Tanaka: "I like the rear view when the car is open – I believe the rear view of a sports car has to be cute! I would also suggest the tail lamps, which are as one with the body. I wanted them to resemble a *fundo* [a balance weight from old-style weighing scales], so I shaved a tail lamp housing myself to get exactly the shape I desired."

Miho Long: *"Which would you say was the hardest part of the body design to execute?"*

Mr Tanaka: "To create the authentic originality of Mazda and Japan on the body surface. You will notice that the lines enclose an aesthetic consciousness, giving different feelings depending on the angle from which the car is viewed, just like a *Noh* mask.

"Every time I take up a chisel to create a *Noh* mask, I always respect the traditional simplicity and perfect curves which have been handed down over the centuries. Many different feelings and wishes are held within the mask, their appearance depending on the light and changing shadows. It is very characteristic of the Japanese, and completely different from the Western notion of expressing perfection concretely.

"I also wanted to enclose the rhythms – peace, motion, and silence – which exist in the Japanese heart, into the form of the sports car. For peace, I looked towards a statue of the Goddess of Mercy for inspiration, a truly graceful symbol. For motion, I thought of a wild animal when it's hunting, running fast and accurate, and for silence, the tranquility of nature. I wanted the car to melt into the scenery, reflecting the light over its curved surfaces.

"I wanted to establish a new mould which was dynamic and original, yet distinctly Japanese in its origin – a mixture of sensitivity and modern technology."

an excellent move (Japan's roads are full of these utility vehicles nowadays), but was also pushing for a new model in the Light (or *Kei*) class. The tiny K-car was a proven winner, and, with limited resources available, many in the company recommended that this route should be taken and the LWS project suspended.

Fortunately, this immediate problem was overcome via a joint engineering agreement with Suzuki in relation to the Light Car; Mazda now had the resources to enable it to do the MPV, the K-car (the Carol) and the LWS, but the men in the finance department were still not too happy. America was always going to be the main market for an open sports car, and the value of the yen was making life hard for Japanese exports.

The first major Japanese sports car success in the US market, the Datsun 240Z, hit the shores of America in 1970. The floating exchange rate system was introduced in 1971, and almost immediately the yen began to strengthen against the dollar. By 1972, 300 yen would buy a dollar instead of the 357 needed at the start of the previous year.

With the oil crisis of 1973, the yen was quoted at 253 per dollar before the greenback recovered dramatically. By the end of the 1970s, when Mazda's RX-7 arrived

on the scene, the rate had dropped to below 200 yen to the dollar, and was still moving in the same direction. 1985 had seen the yen moving strongly against the dollar, pushing prices in export markets up to unprecedented levels, which had an obvious effect on sales.

This was not such an easy problem to resolve, as the thinking behind the LWS was that it should be cheap enough to tempt people into buying what was, at the end of the day, something of an indulgence.

In January 1985, AutoAlliance International Inc., a 50/50 venture with Ford, was established in Flat Rock, Michigan. Having a manufacturing plant in the States would overcome currency fluctuations (MX-6 production began in September 1987, followed shortly after by the Ford Probe, and later the 626), but there were no plans to build the LWS there.

With initial sales projections pointing towards 1800 units a year for Japan, 30,000 for North America and around 3600 for Europe, the volume was hardly massive. Careful design, to keep production costs down, would ultimately be the car's saviour (although, luckily, these figures proved grossly underestimated).

In the meantime, progress was slow. MANA eventually completed the S-2 clay in December

1985. When it was officially presented to the Board the following month, Yamamoto was fully behind the LWS idea, saying it had "a smell of culture." Mazda's Managing Director, Takashi Kuroda, also expressed his support, and, for this reason, on 18 January 1986, the P729 was grudgingly given approval. But then there was another delay ...

Kato, who had overseen the project since inception, decided to step down from his position as head of P729, and concentrate his efforts on new ideas within the recently-opened Technical Research Centre. Naturally, this meant a replacement had to be found. Fortunately, Toshihiko Hirai, previously in charge of the Familia (323), made it known that he would like to be considered for the LWS project. Born in 1935, Hirai was well-respected and had a proven record with the successful 323 range. With his vast engineering experience and a spell in the Service Department, he was declared the ideal man for the job and, in February, duly took up his new post as the P729's Chief Engineer.

In the same month, MANA was told it could start on the third and final clay model (the S-3). Work began in earnest in the middle of March, with Tom Matano and Koichi Hayashi responsible for the majority of input, ably supported by Mark Jordan and Wu-Huang Chin.

Matano wanted to develop a family resemblance between the 'faces' of the various cars in the Mazda range – a frontal view that would immediately single out the vehicle as a Mazda. Using BMW and Mercedes-Benz grilles as examples, he went on: "To us, this is a graphical way of identifying the car. It's great if you have a [long] heritage, and so forth, that establishes you in such a way, but at this point in Mazda's development we wanted to upgrade our image ... To achieve that, we wanted to have something like a body language to [distinguish] the Mazda for that time.

"I always look for the movement of the highlights on a car. It's almost like a drama, or a symphony in some cases; like a Jaguar is a symphony. Every moment that lights move on a surface by driving [along], really [tells] the whole story of a car."

Matano dislikes the use of fussy lines and heavy creases in styling. He said: "I often think of water, dropping onto the roof, following the curvature, going down the roof to the pillar, to the bottom of the pillar, to whatever. And every time this water has to think which way shall I go down – if the water has to think that way – the design is not right yet. You know, it's not natural yet.

"Because it's a convertible, the rear end is very important to identify the car. And yet we don't really want to have a spoiler just for the sake of it, so it's there but it's not really obvious."

During May, the project was considered advanced enough to call a joint meeting between MANA staff and a large delegation from Japan. As far as the American team was concerned, the project was finished.

The LWS taking shape in Japan, based on MANA's S-3 clay. The Americans had been worried that Tanaka would drop the pop-up headlights; in actual fact, Fukuda (seen pointing in the background) wanted the headlamps placed under clear covers, but regulations dictated that the pop-up arrangement remained. Note the Minilite-type wheels.

Once the project was moved to Hiroshima, another round of sketching began. Note the 'LWS' marking on the rear panel.

The MX-5 is definitely starting to show through in this proposal sketched by Iwao Koizumi (Chief Designer of the Atenza, or Mazda 6).

A return to Worthing

Once the decision was finally taken to embrace the lightweight sports car, Mazda again turned to IAD in England – this time to produce five complete running vehicles (engineering mules), and nine bodyshells for test and evaluation.

The mules didn't have the PPF brace (all will be explained in due course), but otherwise were similar to the future production models. Significant detail changes were made along the way, including the use of a larger fuel tank (the original was far too small to be practical), and redesigning of the hood.

IAD actually carried out the front and rear crash tests, which the LWS passed with flying colours. After the Worthing phase in the proceedings was completed, a number of IAD staff were sent to Japan to personally explain problems encountered and make the transition as smooth as possible. The Mazda roadster was now a reality.

The synthesis of man and horse

The author's point of view regarding sports cars has always been that they have only one main purpose – to be driven. Of course, some of the more exotic designs can be looked upon as works of art – like automotive sculpture – but basically speaking, a sports car is intended simply to provide driving pleasure.

The LWS project's Chief Engineer, Toshihiko Hirai, felt exactly the same way. The Japanese love their cars; they represent personal space in a crowded city, something they can own. Few young people are in a position to buy anything in the housing market other than a tiny flat, as prices are extremely high. Even if somebody does take on a mortgage, repayments often continue well into the third generation of the family! The car is also a way to escape into the countryside, or a means of getting to the fishing port. In other words, even given the prospect of enormous traffic jams at certain times of the day, the automobile is considered

Work on a scale model of the Mazda sports car. Shunji Tanaka (left) makes a point, while Satoru Akana (one of the Hiroshima-based designers, seen here on the right) looks on.

Shunji Tanaka (in the foreground, on the left) checking on progress. The scale model in the background, complete with removable hard-top, was a masterpiece.

a necessity to the enjoyment of life. However, a sports car is not just a means of transport: it has to look and feel special, and make its owner enjoy each and every mile, every corner, every gearchange.

Hirai gathered around him a team of about ten people, including Shinzo Kubo (who had been at MANA for a while, and would later become Hirai's assistant), Kazuyuki Mitate and Hideaki Tanaka (both of whom had been with the project for some time), Takao Kijima and Masaaki Watanabe. Hirai, described by Bill Livingstone as "a very professional engineer," began by listing every minute detail that he expected from a sports car, declaring he would

not be happy until this criteria had been met. The list took on an almost legendary status once the journalists got to hear about it!

The concept was originally described as the synthesis of man and vehicle, but this was later changed to the synthesis of man and horse; Hirai wanted the new Mazda to give the driver the feeling of oneness that exists between a good rider and a Thoroughbred stallion.

The final design
The third MANA clay (S-3), arrived in Hiroshima in July 1986, at a time when the studio was packed with other projects. A now familiar figure entered the story when Shunji Tanaka of Design Department No.1 (Hiroshima), took over as Chief Designer. Initially, Tanaka struggled to find a surface plate for the clay; considering the project had still not secured the full support of everyone at Mazda, in a country that is usually so organised, one wonders if this had not been planned to delay it still further. However, one was eventually obtained and, in November that year, Tanaka started work on the model.

Tanaka decided that the car was too heavy-looking for his liking. As he said, he proceeded to "take one layer of skin off the MANA model from front to rear" to reveal a lither profile. He insisted that the wheelbase be shortened slightly, causing more than a few problems for the layout engineers (MANA had already lengthened it during development of the third clay), the most obvious of which being the need to move the battery from behind the seats to a new location in the boot. The battery then encroached on luggage space, but the stylist stood by his decision. In the end, it helped with weight distribution anyway, so could be regarded as something of a mixed blessing, even though a special lightweight battery was eventually deemed necessary by Hirai.

Tanaka and Hirai had several more arguments during the development of the final model. Tanaka lowered the cowl height but was prevented by the Chief Engineer from going the extra 20mm (0.79in) he really wanted, although he did manage to change the width of the air intake. When Hirai found out after taking a ruler to the model, it was too late to change it!

Mazda thought that the car had to have spirit, incorporating the 'beauty of Japan," so the brief mentioned a hint of Muromachi culture – a great era in Japanese history that brought about the tea ceremony, *Noh* plays, floral art, the Zen sect, and so on. There was very little further intervention from the management and marketing people. Tanaka (who was born in 1947 and joined Mazda in 1971) sculpted *Noh* masks as a hobby, and used them for his inspiration. The simple mask's facial expression doesn't actually change, but as soon as a *Noh* actor wears it, by careful movements the mask can change expression through the use of light, shadow and different angles.

The modeller, Shigeru Kajiyama, had the unenviable

Tanaka's finished design. His modifications actually brought the final shape closer to the original Duo 101 clay submitted by MANA when the project first started. From quite an early stage, Tanaka had removed the black rubbing strip and replaced it with a crease line. From this clay, a glassfibre model was built, which was subsequently sent to America to take part in a clinic.

Three views of the glassfibre model that went to the States to take part in a clinic held at the Pasadena Convention Centre in 1987.

job of interpreting Tanaka's vision to make light dance on the car's profile, regardless of whether it was in motion or stationary. When the clay model was completed, the data was loaded into a computer, and it was found that the LWS had 260 different faces. By comparison, other Mazda cars have around 80 different faces.

After working on the clay model for about three months, in between his other work on the Luce, RX-7 and MPV (considered by Yamanouchi to be more important at the time), a resin mock-up of the body was produced. This was duly sent to California for appraisal at the end of March 1987, by which time Watanabe and his team had sorted out the vast majority of engineering details. Although the staff at MANA were dreading the results (they had been told that Tanaka had been quite brutal with his modifications), they were all suitably impressed, and immediately sent a fax through to Hiroshima to convey their congratulations.

It was one thing to impress your colleagues, but the true test came at a clinic held at the Pasadena Convention Centre, when 245 people were invited to give their views on the anonymous vehicle. It received an overwhelming

'yes' vote, duly echoed by dealers, which was almost certainly a key factor in the decision to finally go ahead with the project. The importers in America were fully behind the car, so everything was now in place, signed and sealed. There was no turning back.

Engine

A rotary engine was dismissed at the start of the project. Managing Director, Takashi Kuroda, said that from a marketing point of view, the rotary was better suited to higher powered prestige models. Cost was also an important factor. Masakatsu Kato was also opposed to the rotary but for different reasons: if an existing unit was to be used, the chassis would require costly modifications to enable it to handle the extra power (which would also add a substantial amount of weight), or a new, smaller engine would have to be built.

Sensibly, it was decided to adapt an existing unit to cut down on development time and costs. The fuel-injected, 1.6 litre, twin-cam engine from the Familia GT was selected, and suitably modified to enable the four-cylinder block to be installed longitudinally, instead of in

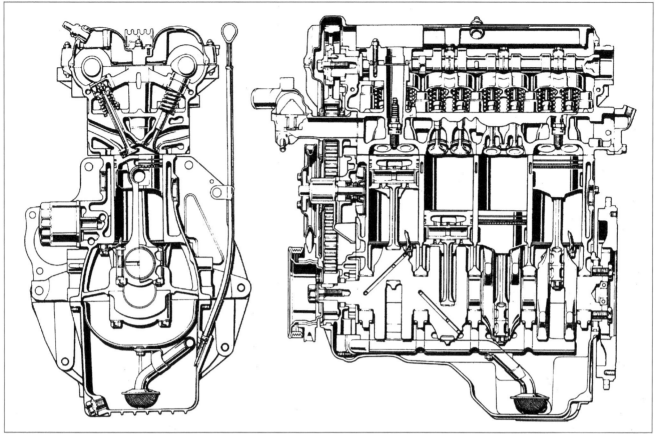

A sectional view of the B6-ZE (RS) engine. Some team members liked the idea of a turbocharged version, but Hirai was determined the car would remain normally-aspirated for a more natural, linear power delivery.

its usual transverse position. Having only recently ushered in the FF layout on the 323 range (which was almost universal on small cars by this time), it is somewhat ironic that this conversion was necessary.

However, the B6-DOHC was found to be less than ideal. Hirai wanted a high- and free-revving engine and, in its standard form, this unit, having been tuned to give low-end torque instead of top-end power, was hardly suitable for its proposed new application. The turbocharged version, available in Japan, was also quickly dismissed.

The water-cooled B6 was therefore adopted by Kazuo Tominaga and his team as the starting point for what would eventually amount to a new engine. The bore and stroke were retained (78 x 83.6mm, or 3.1 x 3.3in), which gave a cubic capacity of 1597cc. The block, with five main bearings,

The engine and five-speed gearbox used in the P729 lightweight sports car.

was of cast iron, while the head was cast in aluminium alloy. Double overhead camshafts remained a feature, operating four valves per cylinder, although the timing was changed to allow higher rpm. The crankshaft, con-rods and flywheel were all subtly altered, and this attention to detail resulted in an engine with a 7200rpm red-line.

But, in typically Japanese fashion, the detailing went much further – even the induction system, cam covers and timing belt cover were stylized to make the engine attractive to look at, and to bear a passable resemblance to Lotus, Alfa Romeo and Fiat twin-cam units! Another novel feature was the cast aluminium sump, complete with cooling fins, in the best Italian tradition.

Fuel-injection was retained, for although twin carburettors would have been nice from an aesthetic point of view (as well as following a traditional sports car line), emission regulations soon scuppered that idea. An L-Jetronic EFI system with a pendant-type airflow meter was employed, and Tsunetoshi Yokokura (who had previously worked on the B6-DOHC engine), designed both the intake and exhaust porting and manifolds. To save weight, the free-flow exhaust manifold was produced in stainless steel rather than the more commonly used cast iron.

Interestingly, instead of using a distributor, it was decided to employ a crank angle sensor, as the old Familia-type distributor would have been in the way of the wiper motor. Although this computer-linked device cost a

fortune compared to the more traditional ignition set-up, it ultimately gave a much smaller and lighter package. Other weight saving measures included the use of an aluminium and plastic radiator which was cooled by a particularly small electric fan.

The new engine was designated the B6-ZE (RS), and with a compression ratio of 9.4:1 produced 120PS (the Japanese measurement of power, which is roughly the same as European bhp) at 6500rpm. Maximum torque (of 100lbft) came in very high up the rev range, at 5500rpm, confirming the sporting nature of the unit. The engine was mounted as far back as possible to bring the weight nearer the centre of the car.

Drivetrain

The gearbox was developed from the proven M-type, five-speed transmission that had seen service in the two-litre Luce and normally-aspirated RX-7. The main changes concerned the shift linkage, which was modified to give a very short stroke between the gears; indeed, when the Mazda engineers had finished, the stubby gearlever travelled just 50mm (2in) from any gear into the neutral position, prompting one tester to compare it to operating a rifle bolt. However, that was not all, as the synchromesh was improved, and a subtle 'click' as the lever reached its stop was built in to enhance the positive feel of the 'box.

After reviewing the specifications on a number of sports cars, close and evenly spaced gear ratios were

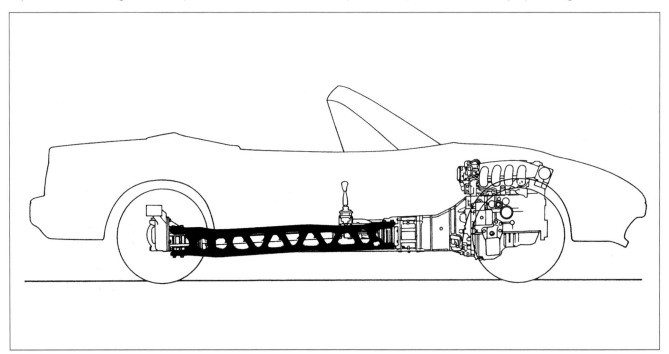

The drivetrain for the LWS was quite short, with the engine mounted a long way back. It was the first car to employ the Power Plant Frame, or PPF. Weighing less than 5kg (11lb), it effectively turned the engine/gearbox and back axle into an integral unit, and made a notable difference in refining power delivery.

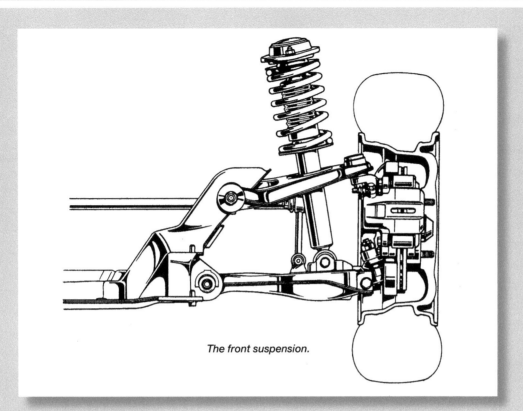

The front suspension.

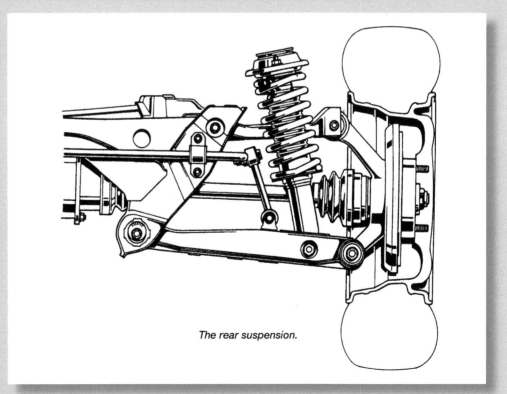

The rear suspension.

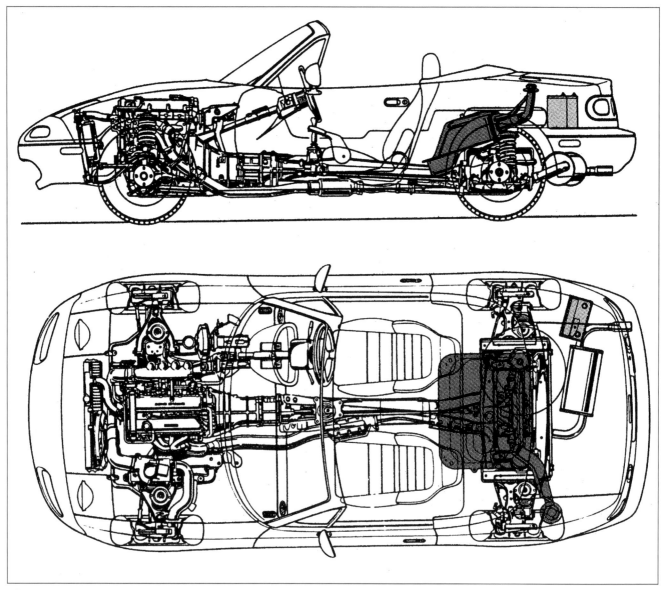

Cutaway drawings showing the layout of Mazda's new sports car. The fuel tank on the NA1 machines, seen above the rear axle, had a 45-litre (9.9 Imperial gallon, or 11.9 US) capacity. One can also see the battery in the boot, put there for balance.

chosen. With a 4.3:1 final-drive, a 3.14:1 first gear gave a maximum speed of 33mph (53kph); the 1.89:1 second gear allowed 54mph (86kph); third, at 1.33:1, gave 77mph (123kph); the direct fourth gave 102mph (163kph), and a 0.81:1 overdrive top, an estimated 117mph (187kph).

The clutch was a single dry plate unit. Power was taken from the gearbox to the back axle via a single-piece propshaft (with the engine located so far back, a two-piece propshaft was deemed unnecessary). A viscous-coupled, limited-slip differential was made available as an option.

Having designed a novel way of bracing the driveline for the forthcoming third generation RX-7, at the end of 1986, Mazda decided to use what it called a Power Plant Frame (or PPF) on the LWS as well. Having tested the idea on an early engineering mule, the system was later adopted for production. The PPF was basically an aluminium bracing piece linking the engine and differential which had been refined and lightened through the use of computer technology; its purpose was to improve throttle response (by stopping the differential unit twisting on its mounts) and reduce drivetrain shudder.

On the subject of throttle response, throttle travel was some 65mm (2.5in) on the LWS, as opposed to the usual 45mm (1.8in) on most Mazdas, thus giving the driver more precise control. The throttle pedal was drilled to evoke memories of earlier sporting machines. Incidentally, an

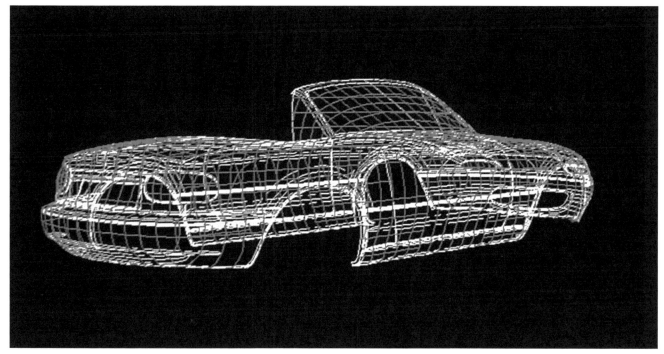

The roadster's body as seen by the GNC-2 computer software.

automatic gearbox was not offered immediately, but was promised for the future.

Chassis

Having originally been under the auspices of the Technical Research Centre, the job of developing the lightweight suspension eventually fell to Takao Kijima and Fumitaka Ando. Kijima was perhaps the ideal person for the job, having thought up the idea of the DTSS system for the second generation RX-7 (the FC model).

It was declared early on that the independent suspension would be via double wishbones all-round. Although it would have saved both time and money to use components Mazda already had in service, unequal length A-arms were unrivalled for sports car suspensions, so a new setup was designed from scratch. Originally, aluminium alloy suspension components were envisaged, but the associated production costs curtailed this line of thought as the LWS was, after all's said and done, supposed to be an affordable sports car. Instead, the A-arms were fabricated from high tensile steel sheet, a material that was strong, reasonably light, and cheap to manufacture.

Up front, a combined coil spring/gas-filled shock absorber sat in between the wishbones on each side; an 18mm (0.71in) anti-roll bar was used. At the rear, Kijima – famous for his perfectionism – allowed the forward lower suspension bush to deform slightly under cornering to give the rear wheel a minute amount of toe-in: an ingenious idea. Again, combined coil spring/damper units were used, along with a 12mm (0.47in) diameter anti-roll bar.

Spring rates were completely different to those of the Familia: 1.6kg/mm at the front and 1.4kg/mm at the rear. The rates for the 323 were quoted as 2.7kg/mm and 2.1kg/mm respectively. Staff from Bilstein spent a great deal of time, alongside the Mazda team in Japan, on the shock absorber settings, thus ensuring the correct amount of damping for the various types of roads around the world.

The pressed steel front subframe not only carried the suspension pick-up points, but the steering gear as well. As the engine was placed so far back, the rack was mounted ahead of it on the front of the subframe. Rack-and-pinion steering was employed, with a ratio of 18.0:1, as opposed to 23.5 on the Familia. This gave 3.3 turns lock-to-lock, but, being such a light car, steering effort remained acceptable at slower speeds. The optional power steering had a 15.3:1 ratio (it was 16.4:1 on the Familia), which translated into just 2.8 turns lock-to-lock.

Drum brakes would probably have been more than adequate for the car's weight and performance (the Porsche 924 had drums at the rear, and drums do provide a better handbrake), but for marketing reasons it was decided that discs all-round would be better.

The Familia was available with this system, and its components provided an ideal basis on which to work. Ventilated discs of 235mm (9.3in) diameter were employed at the front, while solid items of 231mm (9.1in) diameter were used at the rear. The pads had a slightly larger area than those of the Familia, and the servo was

After the Pasadena clinic, Tanaka set about the subtle detailing to make the car ready for production. The tail was made softer, rear overhang was increased by 30mm (1.2in), and the famous door handles at last made an appearance. With so many subtle lines, Naoyuki Ikemizu said the tooling for the panels was very difficult to make. This final prototype had raised 'Mazda' script on the front bumper, and the shield-shaped badge on the nose carried a star above an abstract bird with open wings.

changed to provide the driver with a more progressive feel.

Attention to detail was again much in evidence: The front calipers were at the trailing edge of the discs, with the rear calipers on the leading edge, thus ensuring that the weight of the braking system was kept within the wheelbase. The handbrake mechanism, which worked on the rear discs, featured an automatic adjuster.

Finally, the wheels and tyres also came under the spotlight. While 5.5J x 14 steel rims were the norm, with eight small slots cut into the metal and a tiny centre cap (carrying the Eunos logo in Japan), Shunji Tanaka had come up with an alloy wheel resembling the original Minilite, but given the weight that Hirai wanted, the wheel's would-be manufacturer suggested removing one of the spokes. The 5.5J x 14 alloy wheels were thus destined to have seven spokes instead of eight, and became something of a design icon along the way.

As for the tyres, Mazda approached various companies with a request for a lighter type than those already on the market. Eventually, around 2.5kg (5.5lb) was saved on a set of four 185/60 HR14 radials, with a special tread pattern to deliver enjoyable handling. A spacesaver spare was specified, and placed as close to the rear bulkhead as possible in order to maintain the car's ideal weight distribution.

Body

Hirai once again had very strong views on what the body should be like: "Very light and very stiff." Masakatsu Kato knew that a fibreglass body and backbone chassis, as used on the IAD prototype, was not an ideal recipe for mass-production. This conclusion was not a new one, as Daimler established as far back as 1958 (when it was looking at the details on the SP250 project) that once production reached 3000 units a year, it was cheaper, long-term, to tool-up for steel bodies.

Modern techniques had increased this threshold figure substantially, but the conclusion was basically the same. With high volume sales envisaged for Mazda's LWS, fibreglass was out of the question. Aluminium was also rejected because, although it had an obvious weight advantage, it was a very expensive material compared with steel. However, in Hirai's endless quest for weight reduction, some aluminium would eventually be used for panelwork.

Mazda's GNC-2 computer programme was used to enable the engineers to reduce weight whilst at the same time retaining vehicle rigidity. The car's body was an incredibly light structure, but strength was guaranteed by the thoroughness of Hirai's team. On average, stress measurements are taken and analyzed at approximately 5000 points but, in the case of the LWS project, no less than 8900 readings were used to ensure the body would be free of the problems one usually associates with open cars, such as scuttle shake. Designing the car as a convertible from day one was an added advantage, of course, as converting a coupé into a drophead always involves compromises.

The bodyshell was of all-steel welded unitary construction, although in order to reduce weight forward of the centreline, it featured an aluminium bonnet, while the bootlid was actually made out of thinner gauge steel than that found in the rest of the body. In all, the steel parts of the car accounted for just 16 per cent of the P729's total weight.

The front bumpers were faced with urethane, while the rear bumper used polypropylene. Both were backed by impact absorbing, blow-moulded plastic, and mounted on the bodyshell via lightweight polycarbonate brackets. This arrangement, compared with more traditional bumpers, significantly reduced weight at the car's extremities, thus improving handling. In addition, side impact bars within the doors were tubular to further reduce weight.

The overall dimensions of the roadster read as follows: length 3970mm (156.3in); width 1675mm (65.9in); height 1235mm (48.6in), and wheelbase 2265mm (89.2in). Ground clearance was 140mm (5.5in), while the front and rear track measurements were 1405 and 1420mm (55.3 and 55.9in) respectively.

Although not particularly impressive by today's standards, for an open car the Cd figure of 0.38 was more than respectable, although it did rise to 0.44 with the hood

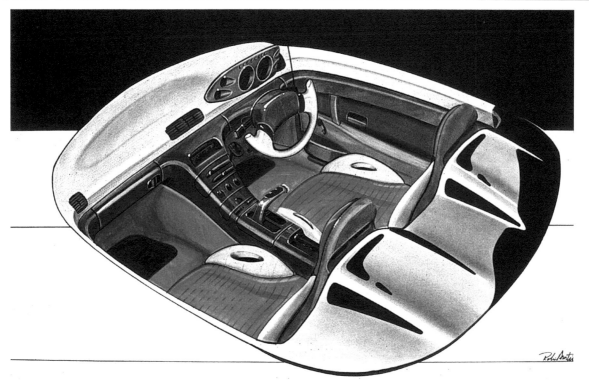

An early interior concept sketch. Note the 'RX' script on the steering wheel – something that appeared on several of the initial design proposals.

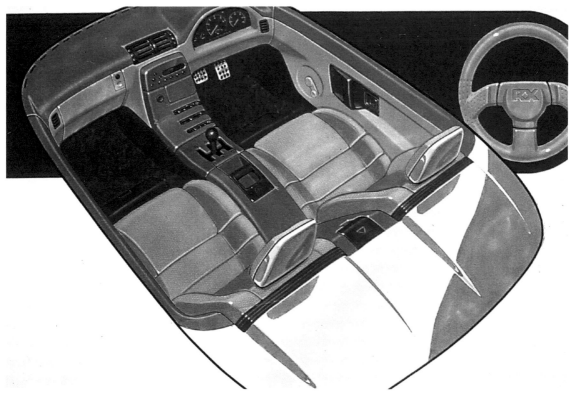

Another early sketch. Attractive, sporting, but far too modern for the new LWS. Something more traditional was sought.

Two of the later designs put forward for the car's fascia.

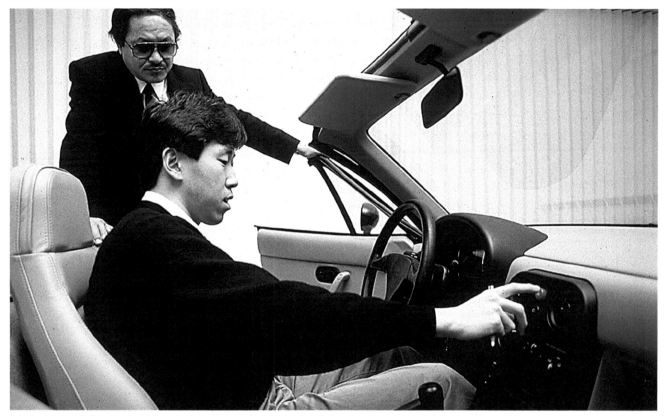

Tanaka and Matsuo assessing an interior styling buck. Inspiration came from traditional-style tearooms.

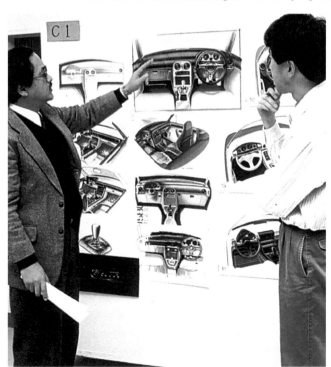

Tanaka-san reviewing interior proposals with Kenji Matsuo (right), the man ultimately responsible for the final cockpit design.

down. Luggage space in the boot, incidentally, amounted to just 125 litres (4.4 cu ft).

Interior

Above all, the cockpit was designed to be functional, and rightly so – it was said to represent the simplicity of a Japanese tea room. Of course, weight was kept to a bare minimum, although the interior was fully trimmed.

Early designs had been a little too futuristic, so Kenji Matsuo decided to resort to a T-shaped theme, like that found on Mazda sports cars from the past. The cluster of instruments contained five main gauges, with a large 8000rpm tachometer on the left and matching speedo to the right. The small oil pressure gauge sat between and above them, while the similar sized fuel and temperature gauges were low down on either side. The two larger dials had chrome surrounds to make them stand out.

In the tail of the T-shaped arrangement were two of the four eyeballs for ventilation (the others were at each extremity of the fascia), and heater controls, both of which were sourced from the first generation RX-7. However, as *Car Styling* said: "The sense of unity has been pursued by fully using the motif of a circle as seen in the meters and ventilator grille, but the basic touch of quality is somewhat unsatisfactory."

High-backed seats with integral headrests were

Dyed-in-the-wool perfectionists.

Visitors to Japan are often struck by the highly detailed and colorful patterns on traditional Japanese *kimono*. The dyeing method, called *yuzen-zome,* is a long, difficult process. First, the pattern is hand-painted on the cloth, which is then soaked in soy milk to prevent blurring of the dye. Then, once again by hand, the dyes are applied and then covered with a rice-paste resist. Once the dye is fixed through steaming, the resist is washed away. While this traditional method is time-consuming, it results in a beauty that's unmatched.

For Mazda, this is a tradition that is alive in our commitment to doing the best job we can no matter what. And Mazda drivers seem to feel the results are just beautiful.

© Mazda Motor Corporation

Mazda advertising from the mid-1980s. Mazda team members were certainly perfectionists regarding the LWS project.

A smiling Hirotaka Tachibana talking over the finer points of the LWS with Toshihiko Hirai (seated). Like Hirai, Tachibana has now retired from Mazda, but works as a consultant for a tuning company (which specializes in MX-5 conversions), and also writes for a number of motoring magazines. Masaaki Watanabe can be seen hovering in the background.

eventually being passed on to Hirotaka Tachibana of the Experimental Department. Tachibana, who had been with Mazda for many years after leaving the Bridgestone concern, wanted a forgiving vehicle that would reward drivers whatever their level of skill. Above all, he wanted the car to feel responsive, and had the suspension tuned so that it performed at its best at around 60mph (roughly 100kph) – a speed that most can enjoy whilst keeping within the law. Testing was carried out at the Miyoshi Proving Ground, as well as on the roads of America and Europe.

In the Psychoacoustics Lab in Japan, a large number of people were asked their opinion of various exhaust notes. Those involved in the tests came from different age groups and backgrounds, representing a fair cross-section of potential buyers. They recorded their thoughts on set format, pre-printed sheets so that the results

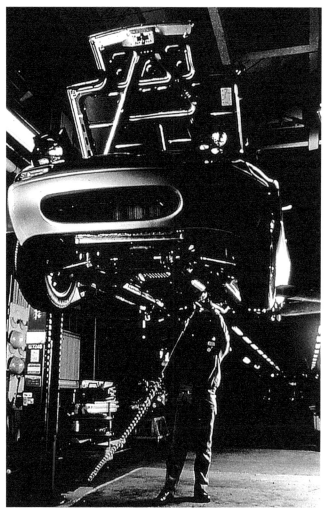

The pilot build at Hiroshima. A small number of journalists from influential magazines were allowed to drive this series of 12 vehicles well in advance of the launch.

selected. Many magazines (and even a few people within the company) commented on the somewhat tight, 'cosy' feel within the cockpit, but most testers were happy with the support provided by the seating.

The steering wheel was a four-spoke affair for America (to allow for an airbag), or a three-spoke design elsewhere. A leather-wrapped wheel was available one way or another – either as standard or as an option – in most markets.

On Hirai's insistence, the sunvisors were made to fold in two to stop them showing over the top rail (although eventually a more traditional design was adopted, presumably to save on production costs). At the other extreme, door trims were very basic, and the cheap-looking handles inside were in stark contrast to the Tanaka-styled items found outside. Indeed, Tanaka commented that a lot of effort had gone into the exterior, but the interior had been produced with cost as a prime consideration.

Finishing touches

By September 1987, drawings had been submitted to enable trial manufacture, with the resulting prototype

The new Mazda sports car with (from left to right), Shunji Tanaka, Mark Jordan, Wu-Huang Chin, and Tom Matano. It was to be known as the Eunos Roadster in Japan, the MX-5 Miata in the States, and the MX-5 in all other markets throughout the world.

could be analyzed effectively, thus giving the engineers a good idea of what the public expected the ideal sports car to sound like; Makoto Shinhama designed and built an exhaust system out of stainless steel to suit. In line with Hirai's drive to keep everything as light as possible, including the standard three-way catalytic converter, the system weighed less than 18kg (40lb).

As well as having the right exhaust note, Hirai stated that a tight seating arrangement was necessary to give the car the intimate atmosphere he wanted. He said: "In the course of development, we are apt to enlarge a vehicle by expecting too much. But then, the sense of unity between the rider and the vehicle is lost. That is why we adhered to limits for all aspects of this car." Even so, he was quick to point out that due to the Mazda's wider track, there was more room in the cockpit than that found in the average British sports car of the 1960s.

The roadster was designed to give the full feeling of an open car. That statement may seem a little obvious, but one only has to think of vehicles like the RX-7 Cabriolet and the Jaguar XJ-S Convertible, where the occupants are cosseted from draughts and direct airflow, and compare them to the wind-in-the-hair experience of a sports car from the 1960s, for instance. Mazda went to extraordinary lengths to get right the movement of air in the cockpit. The large door mirrors were shaped and positioned so that passengers didn't get draughts on their shoulders. It has even been said that a long-haired lady was taken to Miyoshi to see how medium speed runs affected her hairstyle!

Despite having completed its 20-millionth vehicle, as far as the hood was concerned, Mazda didn't have a great deal of experience in this field. The Familia Cabriolet had not been particularly popular, and the introduction of the RX-7 Cabriolet (launched to commemorate the 20th anniversary of Mazda's rotary-engined automobiles) didn't occur until 1987 (the 1988 model year in the States).

It was declared at a very early stage that the hood had to be designed in such a way that it could be operated quickly with just one hand, rather like the hood on the Alfa Romeo Spider. A lightweight frame was duly built, covered with an unlined material which incorporated a vinyl chloride rear window. The latter could be unfastened via a zip to allow for extra ventilation, or for when the hood was lowered. With the soft-top up (or with a hard-top in place), it was found that noise was amplified within the cockpit, but the same is true of virtually all convertibles.

In addition to the standard soft-top (which was found to be both taut and weatherproof in practice), an optional hard-top was made available. An SMC plastic was employed for its construction to give the best combination of light weight and strength, but first attempts were far from satisfactory. Quality and colour matching were improved, but, even then, Mazda was not entirely happy with all the shades proposed, so only red was sold initially. With a glass rear screen, it fixed at six points and made the body noticeably more rigid.

After everything had been finalized, the basic car weighed just 940kg (2068lb); even then, Hirai thought it

was possible to shed more weight. However, Hirai must have been pleased with the weight distribution – most of it being low down and within the wheelbase, just as he wished – with 52 per cent over the front wheels and 48 per cent over the rear. It was an almost perfectly balanced car.

The MX-04

At the 1987 Tokyo Show, Mazda displayed the MX-04. The MX-02 and 03 had been practical cars with seating for four, featuring advanced, but nonetheless conservative, styling. The MX-04 was completely different. Powered by a 150bhp rotary engine, the MX-04 could be fitted with any of three fibreglass body styles: a closed coupé or a choice of two roadsters.

Although the MX-04 was not the prettiest car ever produced by Mazda, some of its features were clues to the future that few picked up on: independent suspension by unequal length upper and lower arms, and a backbone chassis developed by Masakatsu Kato. It is interesting that the headlights on the MX-04 were fixed rather than pop-up, giving the car a similar frontal aspect to the second generation MX-5.

Another debutant at the '87 Tokyo Show (the last to be held at the Harumi site) was the mid-engined Suzuki R/S3. This was the second time in a row that Suzuki had displayed an LWS as its concept car design, and on both occasions they looked suitable for production, giving Fukuda more than a little cause for concern. Maybe Mazda would have a competitor in the near future?

In fact, Mazda knew it was guaranteed at least one competitor, as Ford (which owned 24.5 per cent of Mazda at the time) was planning to bring out the Mercury Capri, a fwd convertible, using a large number of components sourced from the Familia. Based on Ford's Barchetta, an exhibit at the 1983 Frankfurt Show, it was built in Ford's plant in Australia. Although announced early in 1988, it wasn't introduced until the end of 1989.

The pilot build

The Mazda team must have held its breath when Bitter announced a two-seater convertible at the 1988 Geneva Show. It looked very similar to the P729 and was said to be ready for production, with sales to the US in preparation. Fortunately for Mazda, it was a typical Bitter product – upmarket (and therefore expensive), powered by a large Opel engine, and very low volume.

Shortly after this, the pilot build process began, with 12 cars put together by hand at the plant in Hiroshima. These were labelled S1-1 through to S1-12 and would be the vehicles tested by a select number of journalists well in advance of the launch.

Dennis Simanaitis of *Road & Track* was one of those lucky enough to be chosen to test the three vehicles Mazda had provided for the day. "Last summer," he said, "I was invited to Mazda's Miyoshi Proving Ground to drive a prototype of the company's all-new lightweight sports car ...

"It helped assess how brilliantly conceived and executed this new car is. Its convertible top is a good example. It had to be easily erected or stowed from the driver seat. It required a latching mechanism that was easy to use. Erected, it had to offer perfect sealing up to 80mph. Down, it had to stow completely below the car's rear deck line. These engineering criteria give a perfect description of the Miata's soft-top, developed in conjunction with the British design specialist, IAD. Its latches, for instance, are large and of a novel over-centre sort that don't need Godzilla for actuation. Though not a heavily padded top of the Germanic idiom, Mazda does get its top materials from the same firm supplying Volkswagen and BMW ...

"Twist the key and you're rewarded with a pleasant burble from the Miata's 1597cc fuel-injected inline-four, essentially the same dohc four-valver powering sporty 323s. One change, a lightened flywheel, emphasizes its sports car intent ... Snick the shift lever into first, and you'll experience another element on Mr Hirai's list. The shifter and its actuation are super short and wonderfully positive ...

"Consulting Mr Hirai's

MX-5 production at the Hiroshima Plant Complex, where the model was built alongside the RX-7 and a number of other cars in the Mazda range.

list again, engineers worked for a feeling of directness between throttle and rear wheels. I believe a lot of this driveline integrity is achieved by an artfully cast piece of aluminum that connects the engine, transmission and final-drive. Check off another goal successfully met. Handling goals occupy a good portion of the list, and it's in this area that the Miata impresses me the most. Its combination of communication, responsiveness, predictability and forgiveness makes it the best-handling two-seater I've driven in recent memory – and my memory for such things is good ... It was an absolute delight and my post-drive debriefing with Mazda engineers probably sounded like over-hyped ad copy ..."

In Japan, the June 1989 edition of *Car Magazine* noted that "although from the outside it looks like a British lightweight sports of the 1960s, in the way it performs, it is definitely a car from today. After driving it, one is left with a feeling of happiness."

In the meantime, importation and distribution of Mazdas in the States was consolidated with the establishment of Mazda Motor of America Inc. (MMA), and the completion of the Mazda R&D of North America Inc. facility in Irvine, California (MRA, nee MANA). Unfortunately, despite Mazda's best efforts to keep the new car under wraps until its official launch, the cover of *Auto Week* carried a picture of the P729, as well as an article inside; this was at the end of November – a long way ahead of Mazda's planned publicity campaign.

What's in a name?
Throughout the development of Mazda's new sports car, it had been given a number of codenames and designations. Firstly, it was known simply as the LWS, but, as time passed and the LWS was declared an official 'OGG' project, it was given the code P729. Interestingly, despite the second generation RX-7 having already been granted production status, and the fact that work on it was started well in advance of P729 (so one would expect a lower number), it was given the code P747.

Whatever, as P729 took shape, a number of prototypes were built. The first full-size clay produced by MANA was christened the 'Duo 101' by the Americans, but should probably be called the S-1 to comply with future policy.

The handbuilt machine constructed by IAD was designated V705, the V denoting that it was a one-off prototype. Shortly after, the second full-sized styling clay produced at MANA was christened S-2, and the final one, naturally, was S-3, after which, the project was sent to Hiroshima.

The engineering mules, also constructed by IAD in England, were known by the code M-1, the M denoting mechanical. Still using the P729 code, the project was taken through its final stages in Hiroshima until 12 handbuilt prototypes were constructed in 1988. These

were named S1-1, S1-2 and so on up to S1-12, but should not be confused with the MANA styling clays.

It would seem reasonable to expect that, once the new sports car reached production status, things would become simpler. However, three different names were chosen for the various markets.

The MX series of concept cars (the MX-02 Show Car in 1983, followed by the MX-03 in 1985 and MX-04 in 1987) had the right image, and the LWS was so unlike the rest of the Mazda range that a new designation was needed anyway. The new sports car was therefore christened the MX-5 (presumably MX-05 was dropped as it fails to roll off the tongue quite so easily).

So, the MX-5 was the name used in all markets – I'm afraid not! Both America and Japan decided they needed something different. In the USA, Laguna was a hot favourite, but then marketing boss Rod Bymaster came across the word 'meed' in the dictionary. Today, this means 'a reward' or 'due amount of praise,' but Mazda Meed just doesn't appeal. However, apparently its origins lie in an old German word – Miata. It was perfect; the new Mazda would be christened the Miata. However, there was a slight problem – in Japan there was a company with a very similar sounding name.

The Miyata business was founded in Tokyo in 1880, concerning itself mainly with the production of armaments. Although better known nowadays as a manufacturer of bicycles (the company has been in the trade for over a century, after all), Eisuke Miyata had also built a small two-cylinder car as early as 1909. Just before the Second World War, a number of Asahi light cars were constructed, and the company was heavily involved with motorbikes, too. Having produced its first Triumph-based machine in 1913 (also known as the Asahi), it finally stopped building motorcycles in the mid-1960s.

After some negotiations, it was finally agreed that the official designation would be 'MX-5 Miata' in the States, but the home market would use yet another name. On 4 April 1989, Mazda set up the Eunos and Autozam sales channels to augment those already in place. This splitting of the line-up is common practice in Japan where home market ranges are so extensive (Toyota currently lists 45 basic models, for instance, before moving into commercials). Basically, it gives the dealers the opportunity to compete in different market sectors.

Anyway, after much deliberation, it was decided to call the new sports car the Eunos Roadster and to sell it through Eunos dealerships. The word Eunos, apparently, comes from a combination of the latin word for joy and an abbreviation of numbers. Expressed another way, it could be taken to mean a collection of joy! At last, the LWS had proper names for all markets.

Kenichi Yamamoto had been talking publicly about an 'entry level' sports car from as early as 1985 but, in reality, few were prepared for a car like the MX-5. Perhaps they

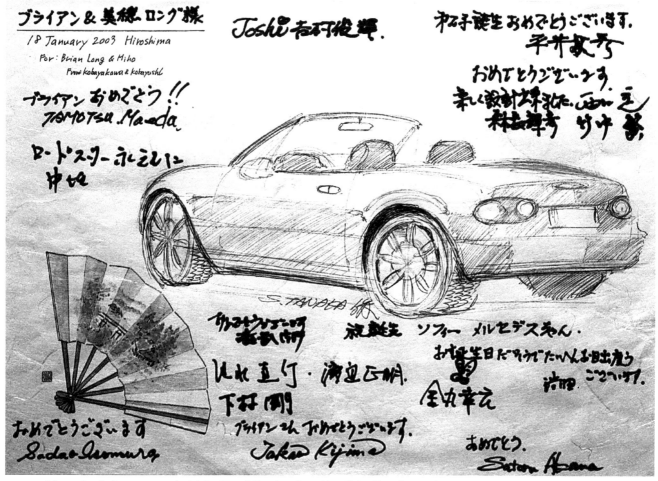

A Long family treasure – a sketch by Shunji Tanaka, signed by all the First Generation MX-5 development team members.

shouldn't have been, for in his 1985 New Year speech, Yamamoto noted two key points. Firstly, that a car should be more than just a tool – it should be something that enriches a person's life. And secondly, a Mazda should always possess a functional beauty. In many ways, the little roadster could be classed as a shining example of Yamamoto's way of thinking.

As will be gathered from this chapter, however, littered with budget and staff shortages, and even a lack of facilities at one point (early development had to take place in a fifth floor office above the design centre garage dubbed 'The Riverside Hotel'), the MX-5's gestation period was far from smooth and straightforward.

Looking back, Toshihiko Hirai said: "There were times when a small breeze from the wrong direction could have blown the project away," but the future of the car that meant so much to him was now secure, and three months ahead of schedule.

Production took place at the Hiroshima Plant Complex (opened in November 1966), where it was built alongside the RX-7 and a number of other cars in the Mazda range.

Chapter 3

Launch of a Legend

After years of preparation, the Mazda MX-5 was finally unveiled at the 1989 Chicago Auto Show in the United States. The event, which opened on 10 February, saw the debut of two other important Japanese cars – the Nissan 300ZX and Honda's NSX supercar – so some of the initial impact could so easily have been lost. However, at less than $14,000, the Miata was in a completely different price bracket, so a clash was therefore avoided.

To help the Miata get even more press coverage, the so-called 'Club Racer' was shown alongside the production models. There was a link here with the launch of the original RX-7, when Toyo Kogyo had put a 'competition version' of the new car on display. This was something that nobody seemed to pick up on, presumably because they were too busy filling column inches on the latest Mazda to look at the past. Finished in a bright yellow hue, it seemed that every magazine in the country featured at least one picture of the Club Racer.

The production models were the most important to Mazda, of course, as it was these that would give the company a return on its investment. The marketing was extremely clever – well co-ordinated and, above all, very thorough. The American public was bombarded with Miata stories; people couldn't even sit down for a quiet evening in front of the TV without seeing one. One American advert showed ghosted images of an Austin-Healey and Triumph TR in the dark. Then day broke with a new, bright red MX-5 sitting in the sunshine outside the garage. The advert implied, with a touch of subtle humour, that the owners of classic British cars more often than not had to contend with the hassle of maintaining or repairing them, sometimes well into the night, whereas the Mazda owner just got into his car and drove away. As Bob Hall once said, although the British sports cars of the 1960s had a certain charm, reliability was not a strong point ...

Although the Mazda didn't officially go on sale until July, by mid-1989, *Road & Track* was already naming the Miata as one of the world's best cars, lined up alongside the Ferrari Testarossa, Mercedes-Benz 300E, Chevrolet Corvette ZR1, and Porsche 911 Carrera 4. In one paragraph, the MX-5 project was perfectly summed up: "Just born and already a star. What does that say about the MX-5? That it stole the hearts (and votes) of nine smitten staffers. That, in typical Japanese fashion, Mazda has done its homework and come up with a design and a concept that time has all but forgotten: the basic, front-engine, rear-drive, open-top affordable sports car." Shortly after the launch, the same magazine had said: "Mazda hopes to attract 40,000 buyers per year, which sounds a bit optimistic." But the timing was perfect; the Hiroshima concern had beaten the competition in a market many thought had disappeared.

Miata fever seemed to grip the States. As *Road & Track* said: "More than any other car in recent memory – and even fairly distant memory – the Mazda Miata has created a stir of almost embarrassing proportions ..." Deposits

Coming: July 1989

The enthusiast's dream come true–again.

Cover from the American pre-launch brochure, describing the car as "The enthusiast's dream come true – again."

Coming: July 1989

Miata
Mazda MX-5

The enthusiast's dream come true–again.

The rear of the pre-launch brochure, aptly showing the tail of the Miata. There were actually two different rear panels to suit the shapes and sizes of registration plates for any given market.

were being taken months in advance, and rumours soon spread of people paying ridiculous premiums. It was a re-run of 1970, when the Datsun 240Z first hit the American scene. Demand outstripping supply was the root cause once again, as only 20,000 units were scheduled for the US in the first year.

The American market was given the 1.6-litre twin-cam engine (much the same as that found in other parts of the world), with a five-speed manual gearbox. Introduced at $13,800 (although few people managed to get one for that price), one of the few standard features that made a concession to modernity was a driver's side airbag, but that was the way things were intended to be with the MX-5 – a full set of instruments and comfortable adjustable seats were far more important. One journalist remarked that the MX-5 was "a refreshing throwback to simpler times."

The basic list price was indeed low. Mazda promoted its new convertible with the phrase "The Return of the Affordable Sports Car." The RX-7 now ranged from $17,000 to a mighty $26,000. On the other hand, if one

looks at the other two Japanese sports cars launched in Chicago, the Z-cars had become progressively more and more expensive (the Z32 type 300ZX was launched at $27,300 in its cheapest form), and the NSX made the Z look a snip, even at that price.

A number of options were available for the MX-5. For starters, there were two different packages: Package A, priced at $1145, included alloy wheels, a Panasonic stereo radio/cassette, leather-trimmed steering wheel and power-assisted steering, while Package B (at $1730) included everything in Package A plus cruise control, headrest speakers and electric windows.

Air conditioning, a limited-slip differential, a CD player and fitted overmats were offered separately. The air conditioning was $795, while the LSD was a very reasonable $250. The CD, listed at a hefty $600, reflected the fact that this type of stereo equipment was then quite novel in a car; the floor mats were just $59.

A number of dealer-installed accessories were available, including a tonneau cover, a protective front-

INTRODUCING MAZDA MIATA.
IT NOT ONLY GIVES YOU A GLIMPSE OF
THE '90S... IT TAKES YOU BACK, AS WELL.

IT IS A CAR THAT INSTANTLY EVOKES A RUSH OF EMOTION. FOR IT IS, AT ONCE, AN AUTOMOBILE OF BOTH CLASSIC FORM AND VISIONARY TECHNOLOGY.

INTRODUCING THE ALL-NEW MAZDA MX-5 MIATA. A CONVERTIBLE. A TWO-SEATER. A TRUE REAR-WHEEL-DRIVE ROADSTER. IT IS AN AUTOMOBILE BUILT WITH JUST ONE OBJECTIVE IN MIND: SHEER EXHILARATION. AND FOR LESS THAN WHAT YOU MIGHT EXPECT, YOU CAN DRIVE ONE OF YOUR OWN. AT THE HEART OF ITS UNIQUE ABILITY TO STIR THE EMOTIONS IS A 16-VALVE, FUEL INJECTED ENGINE. SHORT THROW FIVE-SPEED TRANSMISSION. PLUS A

RACING-INSPIRED 4-WHEEL DOUBLE-WISHBONE SUSPENSION SYSTEM. AND 4-WHEEL DISC BRAKES. A DRIVER'S-SIDE AIRBAG SUPPLEMENTAL RESTRAINT SYSTEM (SRS) IS ALSO STANDARD.

MAZDA MIATA. IT'S DESIGNED TO NOT ONLY PERFORM RIGHT, BUT ALSO FEEL RIGHT. SO DISCOVER THE PURE FUN AND PASSION OF DRIVING A MAZDA MIATA. IT NOT ONLY GIVES YOU A GLIMPSE OF THE '90S... IT TAKES YOU BACK, AS WELL. FOR MORE INFORMATION, CALL THIS NUMBER: 800-424-0202 EXT. 705.

mazda
IT JUST FEELS RIGHT.™

Advertising for the Miata, whether it was on the television or in newspapers and magazines, was quick to point out the concept of the new Mazda – returning the owner to the simplicity of the fifties and sixties, but in a modern, more reliable package.

end mask (known affectionately in the States as a 'bra'), front and rear spoilers, side skirts, trim rings to brighten up the steel wheels, a luggage rack for the bootlid, and various alarm systems.

A removable hard-top was also listed (at $1100), but sold in red only after Mazda had trouble matching the blue and white pigments initially – these shades eventually followed in spring 1990. On the subject of colour schemes, three colours were available in the States: Classic Red, Crystal White and Mariner Blue. Yellow and British Racing Green were expected to join the line-up in the future, but it was a silver hue (Silver Stone Metallic) that made it to the marketplace first.

Press reaction in the States

The July 1989 edition of *Road & Track* carried an article that was to set the scene across the whole of America. One journalist after another seemed to fall under the MX-5's spell: "The Miata's fuel-injected 116bhp dohc four (the only engine Mazda offers) keeps giving all the way up to its 7000rpm red-line. Musically, the engine is a perfect tenor, serenading the driver lustily to 6200rpm, where the exhaust note begins to sour. This engine is mated exclusively (no automatic transmission offered) to a terrific five-speed manual with super-short throws and a precise feel."

The magazine managed a 0-60 time of 9.5 seconds (around a second slower than the Toyota MR2 or Honda's CRX Si), whilst top speed was recorded at 117mph (187kph), and the standing-quarter covered in 17.0 seconds (with a terminal speed of 81.5mph, or 130.4kph).

These figures were nothing more than respectable at the end of the day, but Mazda looked at all-round performance, not just 0-60 times. This policy is one that Porsche has always adhered to – making a complete package

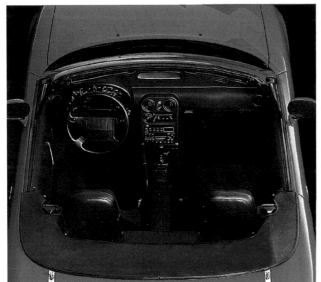

A page from the first American catalogue, clearly showing the snug cockpit of the Miata, and the standard driver's-side airbag fitted to US-spec cars.

The Club Racer was displayed alongside the production models at the Miata launch in Chicago. Apart from the obvious body changes, the Club Racer also featured a modified exhaust system.

Rear three-quarter view of the so-called Club Racer.

Club Racer

In addition to the production models, Mazda decided to show a Miata-based car it called the 'Club Racer' at the 1989 Chicago Show. MRA (nee MANA) stylist, Mark Jordan, was credited with the sporty design.

The respected American journal, *Road & Track*, described the vehicle in its May 1989 edition: "In eyeball-splattering canary yellow, it featured fat Yokohama tyres (205/50 ZR15 front, 255/45 ZR15 rear) faired into sweetly Coke-bottled sheet metal, a plastic rear cowl cover, six-inch spoiler and teensy headlights under plastic covers. Shocks were Bilsteins, body coloured wheels were real/fake Minilites by Panasport. Dee-lish."

The interior was also modified, including leather trim, high back seats (with the Miata logo and racing harnesses) and a Momo steering wheel. In effect, the aftermarket industry started on the very day the car was launched!

rather than a vehicle that is simply quick in a straight line. In other words, a car has to feel right, too.

In this respect, the Mazda team had succeeded. Like every magazine in America, the engineers were more than happy with the overall package. Compared to the competition, it was said "The Miata's four-wheel disc brakes don't seem to give it any relative stopping advantage, either. The brake feel is very good, however, with excellent communication between the pedal, brakes and tyres ...

"We even had the convertible top up one time to check on the headroom (we found plenty) ... The top's sealing against rain and wind noise was superb. With the top down, the swirling winds wafted freely through the driving compartment, but did so without buffeting the occupants to distraction or noisily ruining conversation. It is also important to point out that chassis flexing, a crucial consideration (and problem spot) on convertibles, was virtually non-existent in the Miata ..."

Hailing "the return of the honest sports car," *Car & Driver* was equally enthusiastic. "If the new Mazda MX-5 Miata was any more talented and tempting, buying one would be illegal ... The Miata delivers an overload of the kind of pure, unadulterated sports car pleasure that became all but extinct 20 years ago."

Although probably just a touch biased as a member of the MANA organisation, Bob Hall summed up feelings generally when he described his first drive home from the office: "The very first time I drove a Miata home was kind of an interesting experience. Normally my ride home is about 28 miles, and it takes me 35 to 40 minutes. I stretched it out just a little bit that evening – I think it went to about 137 or 138 miles!"

As for the bodywork, Mark Stehrenberger carried

"JUST BORN AND ALREADY A STAR..."

Road & Track editors in their July 1989 issue named the new Mazda Miata one of their five "World's Best Cars"—extraordinary praise in the company of some of the most exotic and expensive cars in the world.

"Just born and already a star. What does this say about the MX-5? That it stole the hearts (and votes) of nine smitten staffers ... what a sports car should be ... Pure, simple, undistilled, clear-eyed driving fun ..."

Road & Track, July 1989

"Wait till you drive the Miata! You'll love it ... Twist the key and you're rewarded with a pleasant burble ... torque is strong across a wide band ... a feeling of directness between the throttle and rear wheels ... Its combination of communication, responsiveness, predictability and forgiveness makes it the best-handling 2-seater I've driven in recent memory ... The lightweight sports car is back!"

Road & Track, March 1989

"This car is *alive*. It breathes and flexes its muscles and generally behaves more like an organism than a machine ... a flat-out blast to drive. Nimble, precise, even, smooth-wonderful traits all wrapped up into one neat little package ..."

Autoweek, May 22, 1989

"The best sports car buy in America ... the appeal of the Miata knows no bounds ... clean, elegant design ... marvelous road manners ... a real sense of excitement as the revs rise ... a serious for-real sports car that churns up all sorts of memories of late, great roadsters. The only difference is that this one's a far better, more capable car."

Motor Trend, July 1989

"The Miata MX-5 feels just about perfect, delivering every bit of simple fun its voluptuous, organic shape promises ... a car for those of us who were born too late for the English roadster craze ... light, agile, and quick, with a seat that supports, a wheel that commands, a shifter that snaps, and an exhaust note of sheer exuberance."

Automobile Magazine, March 1989

"If you were reading this magazine 30 years ago ... no one would have dared dream of a two-seater so deft in its execution ..."

Car and Driver, March 1989

Shown with optional front air dam, rear spoiler and skirt.

Another double-page spread from the first catalogue issued in the States (printed in July 1989). As the heading proclaims: "Just born and already a star ..."

A 1990 model year Miata, which was the name given to the MX-5 for the American market. Note the optional seven-spoke alloys.

The 1990 model year Miata with optional hard-top in place. In the USA, the hard-top was only available in red but, in the author's opinion at least, it was a very attractive package.

out an expert and in-depth styling analysis. Finding very few faults, he eventually declared: "It's a winner!"

Of the 263,000 Mazdas sold in the USA during 1989 (Mazda's record sales period in the States at that time), no less than 23,052 of them were Miatas, despite it arriving midway through the year. 1990 was a poor year for Mazda Stateside, but nonetheless, Miata sales still continued to rise, helped, no doubt by the introduction of silver paintwork and the option of automatic transmission, added to the line-up in March. Press reaction had been extremely favourable, and the MX-5 Miata was a far greater success than anyone had anticipated.

Memories of the 'Bubble Time' – eager buyers placing their orders for the new J58G Eunos Roadster. In terms of percentages, Japan's economic growth was running at 5.7 per cent – almost twice the national average of most other industrial nations during this period.

An advert dating from mid-1989, a couple of months before the Eunos sales channel (which also sold some of the Citroën range) became operational.

The home market

Car design was becoming more fashion-driven, especially in Japan, a country very receptive to trends. Booms seem to come and go overnight, but when they do happen, they are extremely intense. The retro-boom seems to have lingered longer than most, however.

Starting in the early to mid-1980s, one of the first car manufacturers to cash in on this particular boom was Nissan, with the March (or Micra) providing the basis for the highly successful Be-1, launched in 1985. After this there was the Figaro and then the Pau. The Figaro proved so popular that, in the end, Nissan had to hold a lottery to decide who could have one!

A number of firms followed Nissan's lead. Even at the 1997 Tokyo Show, there were still dozens of exhibits displaying the retro-look. However, with the retro-boom in full swing in Japan when Mazda launched the MX-5, it meant that timing was not only good in America, but also the home market.

Having been officially announced on 3 July, deposits started being taken two days later, and the Eunos Roadster eventually went on sale in Japan on 1 September, sold exclusively through the Eunos sales channel. Oddly, the full four-day press launch wasn't held until 4 July, despite a number of magazines already covering the car beforehand. The launch took place in Hakone, with the Mazda design team present, along with 15 cars.

The home market had a standard 1.6-litre model (which started on chassis NA6CE-100021), and the so-called 1.6-litre Special Package version, the first of which carried chassis number NA6CE-100022. The basic model (priced at

DIMENSIONS ●Overall length:3970mm ●Overall width:1675mm
●Overall height:1235mm ●Wheelbase:2265mm
●Tread(Front/Rear):1405mm/1420mm ●Ground clearance:140mm

POWER TRAIN ●1597cc DOHC 16-valve engine ●Compression ratio:9.4
●Max. power:120ps/6500rpm(NET) ●Max. torque:14.0kg-m/5500rpm ●EGI
●5-speed manual transmission ●Power Plant Frame

A double-page spread from a pre-launch Japanese brochure. Apart from the tail badges, which were obviously different due to the car's various names around the world, the badge on the nose section was unique to the home market.

1,748,000 yen) weighed in at just 940kg (2068lb) and was indeed basic. The Special Package added 10kg (22lb) and a further 150,000 yen. The Special Package included power-assisted steering, seven-spoke 5.5J x 14 alloy wheels, electric windows, and a Momo leather-rimmed steering wheel.

Major options included air conditioning (150,000 yen), a detachable hard-top (165,000 yen), a CD player (62,000 yen) and limited-slip differential. Other components mentioned at the launch included a wood-rimmed Nardi steering wheel with matching gearknob and handbrake handle (which unfortunately didn't appear for some time), a polished cam cover, chrome door mirrors, and an uprated suspension kit. The 5.5J alloys mentioned earlier were augmented by two types of 6J x 14 wheel – a Mazdaspeed five-spoke design, and a 17-spoke one from the SPA concern.

Interior of the Special Package model, shown here with optional air conditioning and CD player. Unlike America, in Japan, the detachable hard-top was available in either red or black.

高回転型1600DOHC16バルブ＋パワープラントフレーム
ダイレクトレスポンスの快感。

パワーユニットは、最高出力120ps/6500rpm(※ネット)、最大トルク14.0kg-m/5500rpmを発生する1600ccDOHC16バルブ、可変慣性給気採用の軽快な自然吸気エンジンだ。そして、高回転域までスムーズに到達するトルクカーブを得るため、高回転設定のカムタイミング、テーパー化した吸気ポートを採用。レッドゾーン7200rpmまで一気に吹け上がる回転特性を実現している。駆動方式は、軽快なFR。しかも、トランスミッションとデフをリジットに結合するアルミ製のパワープラントフレーム(P.P.F.)を採用。これによるエンジン/トランスミッション/デフの一体化が、スロットルレスポンスをよりダイレクトなものにするために貢献している。

4輪ダブルウィッシュボーン＋オープン専用・高剛性軽量ボディ。
ダイレクトハンドリングの快感。

サスペンションは、4輪ダブルウィッシュボーン。路面に対するタイヤのジオメトリーをつねに適正に保ち、すぐれたロードホールディングを発揮する。また、一周をモーメントの低減を図るため、重量をできるかぎり車体中央の重心点方向に寄せてレイアウト。路面にリニアに対応するダイレクトなハンドリングフィールをより高めている。そして、最新のコンピューター解析技術を駆使したオープン専用設計ボディ。軽量化とともに、オープンボディの宿命である剛性不足をはるかに凌ぐ高剛性を実現した。さらに、アルミ製のボンネットフードやステンレス製エグゾーストパイプ、樹脂製バンパー、小型シールドバッテリーの採用など、軽量化を追求している。

Another double-page spread showing the technical specifications for the home market, as well as the 1.6-litre, four-cylinder engine and the LWS chassis. Note the PPF running down the centre, and the seven-spoke wheel design, chosen because seven spokes weigh less than the eight found on a traditional Minilite rim.

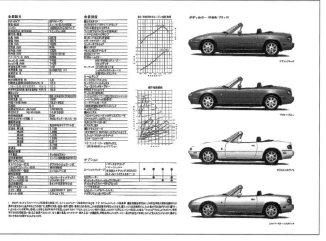

The home market Special Package model, as seen at the time of the Eunos Roadster's official debut. As Car Styling pointed out, the number plate was a little conspicuous, and the use of pop-up headlights perhaps a touch old-fashioned. Although aerodynamics are improved when the covers are closed, the airflow is disturbed when the lights are in use; in addition, the operating mechanism is quite heavy.

The Eunos Roadster with optional rear luggage rack, rear spoiler, and chrome door mirrors.

Part of the first British catalogue for the MX-5, printed in March 1990: 'The enthusiast's dream realised.'

Minor items included polished treadplates with the 'Roadster' logo, a front airdam skirt (provided by the factory in black), projector lamps (situated in the air intake), rear mudflaps, an alloy gearshift gaiter retainer, an alloy handbrake lever handle, and door edge mouldings. Besides Eunos clothing and luggage, perhaps the trendiest accessory was a TAG Heuer 2000 Series watch with the word 'Eunos' stamped into the security clip on the strap.

Reviewing the new Mazda in June 1989, Shigeharu Kumakura of *Car Graphic* thought it was a bit "tail happy" and that the engine could do with a little more refinement, but he immediately fell in love with the interior. The tester also commented on the lack of scuttle shake, the excellent soft-top (claiming there was no real need for a hard-top), and was pleased with the movement of air within the cockpit whilst the hood was down. Interestingly, the feel of the gearshift was highly commended, although the gear spacing between second and third and third to fourth was felt to be not close enough.

In its September 1989 edition, *Motor Fan* pointed out that there were two types of sports car – one that lets you enjoy the sensation of speed, the other the feel of control. The MX-5 fell into the category of driver enjoyment through control.

It was noted that the Eunos Roadster was not a fast car, but the overall mood was good. Little things were very pleasing: "the exhaust note under 4000rpm is very quiet, but over this it becomes musical. The delivery of torque is very smooth, and the whole car reacts to each movement of the accelerator." The tester was also happy with the classical sports car interior, but thought the seats needed to give the driver more support during hard cornering.

Japanese auto-makers always seem to strive for a sports car boot to have at least enough room for two golf bags. The new Mazda was no exception, although after the battery was moved from its original location behind the seats, providing this amount of space was no longer possible. A lack of luggage capacity was one of the few major problems identified by journalists and end users, but Mazda knew the problem existed and would go a long way towards solving it in the future.

It looked as if Mazda had timed the promotional build-up to perfection. Like America, virtually all forms of media seemed to feature the MX-5, and this completely overshadowed the launch of a serious competitor – the Suzuki Cappuccino, a lightweight two-seater powered by a 658cc turbocharged engine. First displayed at the 1989 Tokyo Show, it failed to grab the headlines after the Mazda stole all the glory. For this reason, it wasn't until November

1991 that it finally went on sale. At just 1,458,000 yen, it was very reasonable.

Automatic transmission was added to the Eunos Roadster options list in March 1990. Priced at just 40,000 yen extra, it did, however, add 30kg (66lb) to the overall weight of the vehicle. Factor in the slightly detuned engine (to bring in maximum torque at 4500rpm), and it was obvious that this combination would hardly place the little Mazda in the supercar league, but in a country where most cars have two pedals instead of three, it made a lot of sense to offer the option. A Special Package model was the first to receive the four-speed automatic gearbox (chassis NA6CE-113858), although it was also available on the standard version, the first car being NA6CE-114565.

Available in Classic Red, Crystal White, Silver Stone Metallic, or Mariner Blue, the Eunos Roadster was an immediate hit. From September 1989 to the end of that year, no less than 9307 were sold. In 1990, this figure nearly tripled, with over 25,000 Roadsters finding new homes in the Land of the Rising Sun.

Other markets in 1989

Apart from America and Japan, the only other markets to get the MX-5 in 1989 were Canada and Australia. For many years, Canadian vehicles have usually complied quite closely with American specification models, and the

MX-5 was no exception. Almost 3000 found their way to Canadian buyers in the first year of production, a figure that rose to nearer 4000 in 1990.

As for Australia, its models were very similiar to Japanese spec cars in that both had right-hand drive. By this time, emission regulations were becoming much the same across the world (all countries were stricter than they had been in the 1970s, following the lead of California), so this no longer meant special exhaust equipment for certain markets. In addition, Australia is quite close to Japan (at least compared with America or Europe), so shipping is much quicker.

Sales started in Australia in October 1989 (just one model was listed), and, by the end of the year, 621 had been sold. Naturally, with 1990 being a full year for sales, this figure increased – in fact, by no less than 233 per cent. Shortly after the launch, *Modern Motor* named the car in its 'Best Car Awards for 89/90,' the MX-5 eventually scoring 257 points out of a possible 470 to easily take the title. It was also named 'Car of the Year' by *Wheels* magazine in January 1990, further enhancing the roadster's image Down Under.

Reaction in New Zealand was also favourable. In fact, *New Zealand Car* actually bought an MX-5, citing its good points as "just about everything." However, with a distinct shortage of supplies and strong demand, at one point, as

Early advertising from the UK, which used much the same theme as that in the States, harking back to memories of the sixties – a golden era for sporting machines.

many were being bought 'out of the box' on the 'second-hand' market as from the dealerships, as the thought of a 30 per cent premium tempted a lot of people to sell their car as soon as it was delivered.

The model's first taste of competition came in the Teddy Yip Race of Champions. The event was staged as part of the 1989 Macau Grand Prix weekend, and comprised 16 MX-5s driven by some of the greatest names in motor racing, past and present. Ironically, it was a Toyota Group C driver, Geoff Lees, who took the flag at the finish, narrowly beating Andy Rouse.

The new car in Europe

The MX-5 was making headlines in Europe, too. Writing for *Supercar Classics* in late 1989, Mark Gillies said: "When the Mazda MX-5 hits the showrooms, it should offer all of the [original Lotus] Elan's virtues allied to high (Japanese) build quality, modern (but similar) appearance, far greater refinement and rather more crash protection."

Even *Classic Cars* magazine was enthusiastic: "Here it is! A new popular sports car for the Nineties: the Japanese Mazda MX-5 combines modern engineering with the nostalgic spirit of Sixties sports car motoring, and it costs about the same in real terms as an MGB once did ... At £14,249 we have no doubt there will be a queue of prospective owners chasing the 2500 MX-5s destined for the UK market in 1990."

But the author was a little more sceptical, predicting that the new Mazda was going to find life harder in Britain than it had in the States and Japan. This country has always been extremely slow in warming to the qualities of Japanese cars ... As I wrote in the second volume on the Nissan Z-cars: "At the end of the day, British buyers want a badge, and often pass judgement on a car before they've even seen it, let alone driven it. They also have an image of pricing relative to the marque. If it has the right badge, it's brilliant and excellent value for money – the wrong badge, it's an over-priced heap of junk! In that respect, it is sad to reflect on how little things have changed since the early 1970s."

British taxes on new and imported cars, which seem extortionate compared to America and Japan (and even some other parts of Europe), would negate much of the MX-5's price advantage – a Panther Kallista or four-cylinder Morgan could be had for similar money. The new Elan was expected to cost less than £20,000 (it eventually went on sale at £17,850), a TVR S2 was £16,645, the top-of-the-range Caterham was only £11,570, and the new Reliant Scimitar range started at under £10,000. Besides, the British weather makes the everyday use of convertibles questionable for all but the bravest of die-hard open car enthusiasts, and many would doubtless regard the Mazda as a cheeky impersonator.

In addition, if a drophead can only occasionally be used, why not buy a real old English sports car? The classic car boom was at its height, so spares were plentiful thanks to firms reproducing them, and magazines were packed full of cars for sale. A monthly from the time of the MX-5 launch was advertising a chrome bumper MGB Roadster, fully restored to "outstanding condition" for £9250, while a garage had a Lotus Elan S3 Drophead for £14,000. Both would attract cheaper classic insurance, another consideration.

There was also the new Lotus Elan hovering in the background, which, naturally, got a lot of the limelight in the British press. However, in its guide to the 1989 Motorfair, *Autocar & Motor* said: "Mazda throws down the gauntlet to Lotus as the MX-5 makes an appearance in the UK for the first time. Due to go on sale here this February, the MX-5 will be a crowd-puller as a logical, cheaper rival to the Elan."

The Mazda MX-5 was actually launched on the 14 March 1990 (starting with chassis JMZNA18B200100001). It came with the familiar 1.6-litre twin-cam engine (which in UK spec developed 114bhp) and a five-speed gearbox. Features included power steering, 5.5J x 14 seven-spoke alloys, electric windows, a Momo leather-rimmed steering wheel, black cloth trim, and a Clarion CRH60 radio/cassette unit. It was available in four basic colours: Classic Red, Crystal White, Mariner Blue and Silver Stone Metallic – the same options as those for the home market.

William Kimberley reviewed the car for the April 1990 edition of *MotorSport*, and stated: "Considering that the car will cost £14,249 inclusive of tax and VAT, it is strange that the door mirrors have to be hand-adjusted from the outside, that a clock is not included and that the aerial does not fold down but has to be unscrewed to remove it. The windows, though, are electrically operated. These quibbles apart, the car itself is a charmer. The gearbox is superb, the engine responsive and the sheer joie de vivre of driving it exhilarating."

After recording a top speed of 114mph (182kph) and a 0-60 time of a fraction over nine seconds, *Autocar & Motor* was equally complimentary. It said: "The MX-5 is a total success. Mazda's single-minded determination to provide fun has produced a car of the rarest quality. Above all else it is its ability to involve the driver intimately in its every reaction and response that makes it a joy to drive. Few others, at any price, can offer so much."

The same magazine later carried out a test to find the best-handling car on sale in Britain. Gathering together ten sporting machines and a similar number of drivers (including ex-F1 man, Jonathon Palmer), the MX-5 came away a clear winner. It scored 23 points – eight more than the Porsche 944, and 13 more than the third-placed Ford Sierra Cosworth 4x4.

All of Mazda's attention to detail had obviously paid off and the press loved the car, but this enthusiasm was as nothing if people didn't go into Mazda dealerships (there were 185 in the UK at that time) and part with their money. Fortunately for Mazda, the author's scepticism was unfounded; the MX-5 seemed to create a new breed of enthusiast, one not deeply rooted in the classic car movement and only happy to wallow in nostalgia, but a breed that wanted the fun of an open car combined with trouble-free, reliable motoring.

Other European countries fell in love with the little Mazda, too. Launched at DM 35,500 in Germany, the entire quota for 1990 (2000 cars) was sold in a matter of days.

The end of a perfect year
Toshihiko Hirai summed up the general feeling with: "Some people thought this simple idea was stupid, but the original RX-7 concept has gone too far upmarket. This level is now vacant. We may not make a big profit with this, compared with cars like the 929. There might not be so many of these customers, but they have very strong feelings. It is like seeing your former lover 30 years later."

By the end of 1989, the MX-5 had already picked up a large number of accolades. In the USA, *Auto Week* voted it 'The Most Fun Car,' while *Road & Track* included it in its 'World's Best Cars' listing, where it finished second only to the Ferrari Testarossa; *Automotive News* called it the 'Hit of the Year.'

In its home country, *Sports Nippon News* hailed the Eunos Roadster as the 'Best Sporty Car.' Even *Autocar & Motor* in the UK voted it the 'Best Sports Car' in a review of 1990 models. As the months passed, the awards came thicker and faster, and from all points of the globe. It is doubtful whether a single model has ever had so much praise heaped upon it.

Chapter 4

EARLY PRODUCTION HISTORY

After such a universally warm reception, it was fairly obvious that the MX-5 was destined for success. The popularity of the little roadster took everyone by surprise, and, by the end of 1990, over 140,000 had been built (cumulative production of all Mazda vehicles reached 25 million units at the same time). Forgetting the 12 produced in 1988 during the pilot build, this meant that, in just two years, the MX-5 had already outsold the Alfa Romeo Spider by quite some margin, despite the car from Milan having been introduced way back in 1966!

To the surprise of many people abroad, the Eunos wasn't awarded the Japanese 'Car of the Year' title. However, the model that clinched it – the Toyota Celsior (or Lexus LS400 outside Japan) – was an exceptional motor car and a worthy winner, even more so when one considers the market sector it took by storm. The new Nissan Skyline was another stunner, especially in GT-R guise, and took second place. The Eunos Roadster came third, which was quite an achievement given the competition – Nissan's 300ZX and Infiniti Q45, and the new Toyota MR2 included.

At the 1989 Tokyo Show, a car finished in British Racing Green and sporting a tan leather interior had been exhibited on the Mazda stand to gauge reaction. In July 1990, it joined the line-up in Japan – badged as the V Special – to celebrate the first anniversary of the Eunos Roadster. A variation on the Special Package model, a classic wood-rimmed, three-spoke Nardi steering wheel dominated the driver's view, and the natural theme was extended to the matching wooden gearknob and handbrake trim. A CD player was included as standard, as were polished treadplates with the 'Roadster' logo. Finished in Neo Green with a tan interior (including leather-trimmed seats) and hood cover, it was available with either manual or automatic transmission, and priced at 2,122,000 and 2,162,000 yen respectively.

By the end of 1990, a further 25,226 Eunos Roadsters had been sold, taking the home market total to 34,533 units. In the meantime, the M2 project had been founded in Japan, which brought together a group of engineers and planners to develop MX-5 specials.

The MX-5 in Britain

The 1990 British Motor Show was held at the NEC, opening at the end of September; Mazda occupied Stand 108 at the event. The show saw the world debut of the Gissya concept car – a futuristic MPV that perhaps predicted the forthcoming trend for this type of vehicle. Sadly, it stole quite a lot of the thunder that the MX-5 deserved. Mind you, with a lengthy waiting list only just starting to shorten, it probably didn't need any more promotion.

In the following month, a hard-top became available through the dealer network, having been announced a few weeks previously. Made from glassfibre, it sported a lined interior, heated rear screen, a courtesy light and through-flow ventilation. Priced at £1145, it was produced

A rare shot of MX-5 production. The Mazda sports car was produced almost exclusively in Hiroshima, although for a brief spell during the boom of the early 1990s, it was built at Hofu in the Yamaguchi Prefecture. Once demand subsided, production shifted back to the Hiroshima Plant Complex.

in conjunction with TWR (Tom Walkinshaw Racing) of Oxford, and was listed in Classic Red, Mariner Blue and Crystal White to match car body colours, or Black with a grained finish. There was also a trolley and cover available for owners to store the hard-top safely when not in use.

The official Mazda UK price list dated 5 September 1990 quoted £14,899 for the basic car, with metallic paint adding £175, and air conditioning (a rarely taken-up option in Britain) adding a further £1259 to the bill. At this time, the turbocharged RX-7 coupé was £22,599, while the Cabriolet was £24,999. The most expensive 323 was £13,279, with prices in that range starting at £8469, so the MX-5 wasn't exactly cheap.

Indeed, Roger Bell, writing for *Supercar Classics* at the time commented: "Here is a forward-to-the-past ragtop roadster that epitomises what fun-car motoring is all about. Apart from its indifferent performance, the standard MX-5 is hard to fault dynamically. Explicit steering is so sharp,

The home market's V Special of July 1990. The automatic gearbox option was introduced in Japan four months earlier. A polished cam cover, uprated suspension, and detachable hard-top (finished in body colour) made up the options list.

Studio shot of the V Special, introduced on the home market to celebrate the first anniversary of the Eunos Roadster (Japan's name for the MX-5). Finished in Neo Green, it featured a tan leather interior and a host of extras.

The tasteful interior of the V Special, with its gorgeous Nardi steering wheel.

so accurate that it faithfully obeys commands as if by telepathy. Fingertip delicacy is rewarded with composed balance and precision, just as surely as clumsiness is punished by raggedness. It rewards the sympathetic driver with an intimacy that no other Japanese cars (and few European ones) possess. The neat hood (augmented now by an optional TWR-made hard-top) is even better than an Alfa Spider's. There's only one serious problem with the MX-5. It costs £14,250, which is surely far too much."

In fact, the price was even higher but, nonetheless, by the end of the year Mazda UK had sold 27,598 vehicles, of which, no fewer than 2246 were MX-5s. This was actually quite an impressive figure, for the rest of Europe managed only 7021 sales, and Australia could do no better than 1446 units.

Inspired by the MX-5 race at the 1989 Macau Grand Prix, a one-make series was established in the UK. The 1990 Mazda MX-5 UK Cup was run over 12 rounds, taking in Britain's finest racing circuits along the way,

Action from the final round of the 1990 Mazda MX-5 UK Cup, held at Silverstone. Patrick Watts (who was declared champion at the end of the series) is seen leading Mark Lemmer (runner-up in both the race and the series) and Robert Speak. A total of 27 competitors took part in the MX-5 UK Cup that year.

Mazda wasn't the only company to display the MX-5 at the 1990 British Motor Show, as IAD had one on its stand alongside the new AC Ace. This photograph accompanied IAD's press release dated 20 August 1990.

with all the cars being slightly modified by Roger Dowson Engineering. Patrick Watts was declared champion after dominating the series; he finished on 116 points (32 ahead of his nearest rival). It is interesting to note that Watts was also champion of the Honda CRX one-make series that year, and when Mazda returned to the BTCC scene in 1992 (with the 323F), it was Watts who was chosen as its driver.

The MX-5 BBR Turbo

Although virtually all road test reports were complimentary, not everyone thought the MX-5 was faultless. In a *Classic & Sportscar* article comparing various sports cars, Julian Balme pointed out a number of gripes: "The God-awful positioning of the front number plate, the hideous wheels (if you're going to copy a Minilite, then do it properly), and the flip-up headlights are like surfboards when erect. The other two things I dislike about the car are the steering

The MX-5 BBR Turbo. Although the badging was very discreet, with 'BBR Turbo' added at the end of the existing 'Mazda MX-5' script on the tail (as well as the trailing edge of the front wings), the catalogue described it as "The Ultimate Sports Car of the Decade." The optional wheels were by OZ Racing.

Another view of the MX-5 BBR Turbo. Like the other BBR pictures seen here, this press photograph was actually sent out by the Mazda UK Press Office, confirming the project's official status.

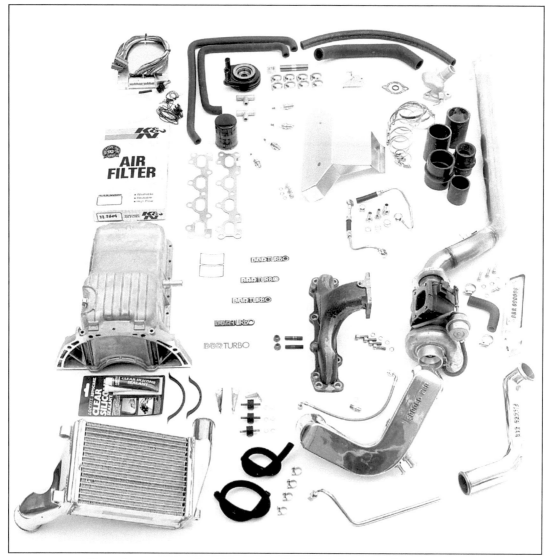

The various components which made up the BBR turbo conversion.

and the lack of excitement emanating from the exhaust system." To be fair, there were just as many aspects of the vehicle the writer did like, especially when he compared the MX-5 to his first generation Lotus Elan.

In the same article, Mike McCarthy had few criticisms, but in the depths of an English winter found that "on slippery, icy surfaces, it was the most lethal of the lot, with zero grip. In any direction." When the final ratings were compiled, the order of merit was as follows: first, the AC Ace, then the Jaguar E-type, Alfa Romeo Spider, Lotus Elan, Mazda MX-5, Jaguar XK120, Chevrolet Corvette, MG TC, MGB, and finally the Fiat X1/9.

Once the honeymoon period was over, by far the most common complaint about the car in Britain was a shortage of horsepower. Mazda UK was quick to try and silence the critics, though, and a press release issued on

8 November 1990 described a new turbocharged version of the MX-5. It stated that the latest model, known as the BBR Turbo, "promises to be one of the most exciting sports cars of the decade." The release continued: "Mazda Cars (UK) Ltd, in conjuction with Brodie Brittain Racing, are proud to present the Mazda MX-5 BBR Turbo – a superbly-designed sports package that retains the handling characteristics of the standard car."

Brodie Brittain Racing of Brackley, Northamptonshire, was recognised as one of the country's leading specialists in the art of turbocharging, with years of experience in the field of motorsport. "The Mazda MX-5 BBR Turbo can accelerate from 0-60 in a blistering 6.8 seconds, and then on to a potential maximum top speed of 130mph [208kph]. Even more impressive is the huge increase in engine power and torque performance – BBR has raised

	Standard MX-5	**MX-5 BBR Turbo**
Power	114bhp @ 6500rpm	150bhp @ 6500rpm
Torque	100lbft @ 5500rpm	154lbft @ 5550rpm
0-60mph	8.7 seconds	6.8 seconds
Top speed	121mph (194kph)	130mph (208kph)

How the standard MX-5 compares with the MX-5 BBR Turbo.

The attractive cover of the 1991 model year Miata brochure. The same picture was also used in magazine advertising in the States; indeed, through the years, many Mazda catalogues have used retouched rather than new photographs to illustrate updates.

the standard 114bhp to a potent 150bhp, and torque has been increased from 100lbft at 5500rpm to 154lbft at 5500rpm – giving a massive 50 per cent boost in mid-range power. The result is that the Mazda MX-5 BBR Turbo can truly claim to be the new high-performance sports car of the 1990s.

"Yet for all of its attributes, the BBR Turbo is also one of the most tractable turbocharged cars available, whether you're motoring in town, cruising on the motorway, or just enjoying its handling and performance through the country lanes on a summer's evening.

"Priced at £2700 (depending on dealer location), the Mazda MX-5 BBR Turbo conversion is available from Mazda dealers throughout the country and is supported by a full three-year Mazda Cars (UK) Ltd warranty."

The car was also offered with a special set of alloy

wheels and Dunlop D40 M2 tyres (priced at £999.95) along with a limited-slip differential costing £620.98. However, Mazda was quick to point out that the package was more than just a case of bolting a turbocharger to the standard car – extensive testing in all conditions had ensured that reliability and economy didn't suffer. In addition to closed circuit testing, more than 6000 miles (roughly 10,000km) were covered on public roads, while the prototype turbo engine ran for 150 hours non-stop without missing a beat.

More than 140 separate parts were used in the BBR conversion, but naturally the most important component was the race-proven Garrett T25 turbocharger. A completely new exhaust manifold, cast in high temperature alloy, and a stainless steel heat shield and exhaust downpipe were fabricated, along with an air-to-air intercooler. Competition spec hoses were used throughout, and the engine management programmes were recalibrated. In fact, BBR actually designed an auxiliary engine management computer to control the fuel-injection, ignition and boost pressure.

The figures at the top of the page comparing a standard MX-5 to the BBR Turbo certainly make interesting reading.

After the announcement of the BBR Turbo, *MotorSport* revealed that: "The brief from Mazda UK was not an easy one, not least because the inside of the engine had to be left well alone. That meant keeping the 9.4:1 compression ratio, unusually high for a turbo engine, and also retaining the pistons, camshaft, etc. In fact, the conversion had to come in a kit form that could be sent to any one of 70 Mazda dealers ... To keep the Mazda warranty, 150bhp is the limit [but] BBR are working on what they describe as a Phase 2 conversion, that pushes out [over] 230bhp, although this comes without the Mazda sanction, and the work can only be done by BBR."

The same magazine also road tested the car, and had this to say: "There is little turbo lag and the engine retains its tractability. The delightful little MX-5 gearbox makes stirring the cogs about an absolute delight, but the engine has a broad enough spread of power to keep that a pleasure rather than a necessity. The 0-60 time is significantly reduced from 8.7 seconds to 6.8 seconds, and the top speed has become a genuine 130mph

[208kph]; a 130mph that in this diminutive, firmly sprung sports car is quite fast enough.

"BBR independently turned their attention to the suspension, and in conjunction with Koni developed some dampers specifically for the MX-5. They tried some four or five combinations before settling on the correct type. These are combined with BBR springs that have a progressive action like rising rate suspension in motorcycles. The first portion of the suspension travel is soft, but the resistance of the springs increases as the deflection increases, so that in quick cornering there is far less roll than on the standard car, but the ride comfort is not unduly sacrificed. There are also anti-roll bars in the BBR kit." The BBR suspension kit was priced at £495 plus fitting, incidentally.

An American update

During 1990, the Miata was named 'Automobile of the Year' by *Automobile* magazine. The car deposited with *Road & Track* had everyone in raptures, although it was noted that,

whilst cold, the engine had a tendency to hesitate and the brakes were a little sharp on the first few applications. Also, after just 9000 miles (14,400km), the hood was starting to show signs of wear. However, there had been no unexpected bills, and only $70 worth of maintenance. Obviously, the title of 'most trouble-free' sports car in the 1990 JD Power Survey was well-deserved.

Despite a poor year for Mazda as a whole in the States, Miata sales were still very strong in 1990, and it seems that *Road & Track* went a long way to explaining why in a comparison test involving the RX-7, Nissan 300ZX, Porsche 944 and Toyota MR2. The journal stated: "For most of us, the job of a sports car is to take pavement – particularly winding pavement – and alchemize it into that elusive thing called fun. This the Miata does better than all the others ... A majority of the group said the Miata would be their first choice if they had to pick one car for the entire trip. A Feature Editor said – 'It has everything I want from a sports car – it's fun, light, quick, agile and it's the cheapest. What more could you ask?'"

The 1991 model year Miata in Mariner Blue. Standard colours at this time included this shade, Classic Red, Crystal White, and Silver Stone Metallic. There was also a limited run Special Edition in British Racing Green. A hard-top could be specified in all these shades, previously listed in red only in the US on the earliest cars.

Cover of the July 1991 edition of Motor Trend magazine.

American advertising from the latter half of 1991.

Tasteful advertising for the Miata Special Edition. Based on the Package B model, each car came with a personalized interior badge.

The same magazine named the Miata 'One of the Ten Best Cars in the World,' and the 'Best Sports/GT' in the $13,000 to $21,000 bracket.

Interestingly, *Motor Trend* had found it hard to choose a winner when it compared the Miata to the second generation MR2 GT, declaring it an honourable draw, but in a similar test in the UK, *What Car?* thought the Toyota was best – just! However, while only 25,000 MR2s were exported worldwide in 1990, American Miata sales for the year added up to 35,944 units; people were definitely voting with their wallets in favour of the Mazda. By this time, the changes for the 1991 model year had been announced.

For the 1991 season, the Miata started at $14,300, and was now available with ABS braking as a $900 option. One magazine stated: "With that single addition, the Miata is just about perfect." Maybe Mazda thought so, too, for other than the new ABS system, mechanical specifications and options stayed pretty much the same as for the previous year.

However, March 1991 saw the launch of the high spec Special Edition. Basically – apart from a few subtle differences (such as the steering wheel) – it was the American equivalent of the home market's V Special.

A dramatic image from the home market's catalogue of late 1991.

Standard colours in Japan included Classic Red, Silver Stone Metallic, Crystal White, and Mariner Blue (by this time, the detachable hard-top was available in all the shades). There were actually three other colours available in 1991 – the V Special could now be bought in Neo Green or Brilliant Black, and the J Limited came in Sunburst Yellow. All cars illustrated here have the Special Package equipment, except the Crystal White example, which is a basic model.

Ironically, the dark green shade was known in the States as British Racing Green, but the Special Edition was undoubtedly an attractive package with tan interior and hood cover, leather-trimmed seats, CD player, polished treadplates, electric windows, a personalized brass plaque and real wood detailing (including a Nardi gearknob) all coming as standard; a matching hard-top was available for $1400. Listed at a hefty $19,249, the automatic transmission option came slightly cheaper than usual, but demand for the BRG car pushed prices well above list in any case. In fact, all 4000 built were sold within just three months.

Looking at the bigger picture, demand waned slightly in 1991. But, considering the price increases and the fact that the Miata was old news by the end of the year, 31,240 sales – less than 15 per cent down on 1990's figures – was actually quite amazing. The Special Edition had obviously helped, but there was no denying that the Miata was still very popular.

The home market in 1991

In July 1991, a minor change was announced. It was found that a 'performance bar' – basically a brace that connected the lower control arm pivot points on both sides – was needed to stiffen the car and strengthen the rear suspension. Chassis NA6CE-150212, built in August, was the first vehicle to receive this modification. Naturally, export models produced after this date inherited the same bracing piece.

Sales of the revised cars began in August. The basic Eunos Roadster (now available in manual guise only) was still listed but never particularly popular. With prices starting at 1,885,000 yen for the manual car (an automatic gearbox added 40,000 yen), the Special Package found a great deal more favour.

The V Special continued, albeit at a slightly higher price – the manual car was now listed at 2,157,000 yen, while the automatic came in at 2,197,000 yen. The Neo Green paintwork was still a feature, but the V Special could now also be bought in Brilliant Black, thus becoming the first roadster on the home market to be offered with black coachwork. Polished kickplates around the door speakers were now a standard fitment on this top-of-the-range model.

At the same time, Japan's first limited edition example was announced: the 1.6-litre J Limited finished in a colour known as Sunburst Yellow. Based on the Special Package, the manual car was priced at 1,900,000 yen,

Beautiful publicity shot of the V Special from July 1991, seen here in its traditional green coachwork, and the new black option (nearest the camera).

The J Limited: Japan's first limited edition model.

Well-appointed interior of the J Limited.

with the automatic listed at 40,000 yen more. Features included the same Nardi steering wheel as that used on the V Special, a Nardi gearknob (on manual cars), wood trim on the handbrake, and stainless treadplates. A hardtop finished in the same colour as the body was listed as an option. The first J Limited carried the chassis number NA6CE-150211, and only 800 were ever built. Amazingly, they were all sold on the first day.

There was a rumour during this period, reported in Australia's *Modern Motor* magazine, that Mazda was testing a turbocharged two-litre version of the MX-5. Given the lengthy lead times associated with magazine articles, it's unlikely this car had anything to do with the recently-formed M2 team, but mention was made of semi-retractable headlamps, a feature later found on a number of M2 prototypes. Whatever, nothing more was heard of the project.

For the 1992 model year a remote bootlid release was placed alongside the fuel filler lever. A total of 63,434 MX-5s were built during the 1991 calendar year, taking the cumulative total to almost 205,000 units. Of these, 22,594 were sold in the home market.

As a matter of interest, the 1991 Tokyo Show saw the debut of two more concept vehicles that would have competed directly with Mazda's Roadster – the Daihatsu X-021 and the Mitsubishi HSR-III. The Daihatsu was perhaps the closest to the MX-5 concept, but neither vehicle went into production. The Subaru Rioma was another worthy debutante, although, had it been given the green light, this high powered, four-wheel drive Targa-top model was intended for a slightly different market sector.

Britain in 1991

The MX-5 one-make series returned in 1991 (again, over 12 rounds), with sponsorship coming from Clarion, Car Line, Dunlop, and Castrol. At the start of the year, David Palmer, Marketing Director of Mazda Cars (UK) Ltd, said: "The introduction of the Mazda MX-5 UK Cup has been tremendously successful. Throughout 1990 we saw some

very close and entertaining racing at every round. With some new competitors involved for 1991, I think the series should be even more spectacular. It promises to be another memorable year."

What Car? magazine voted the MX-5 'Sports Car of the Year 1991,' further adding to the model's bulging trophy case. Then, on 14 March 1991, Mazda UK announced the £18,249 MX-5 Limited Edition to celebrate the first anniversary of the car in Britain. A total of 250 were made available, 25 of which were reserved for tax-free sales or personal exports.

The model was basically another variation on the V Special theme, the British Racing Green paintwork set off by contrasting tan leather seats and a tan interior. Naturally, it came with a very high specification, and featured a wood-rimmed steering wheel, wooden gearknob and handbrake handle, unique 6.5J x 15 alloy wheels, central locking, four-speaker Clarion CRX111R radio/cassette, polished treadplates, a clock, and leather-trimmed overmats.

The press release read: "Each car will only be available in traditional British Racing Green and will come with a certificate of authenticity, stating that it is a Limited Edition MX-5, together with an individually numbered and engraved brass plaque mounted on the dashboard. To make each car even more personalized, a special leather owners' wallet bearing an identical plaque to the one fitted to the car is included, along with a specially embossed leather keyfob."

David Palmer stated: "Following the successful launch of the Mazda MX-5 last year and the tremendous reception it received, we felt that a Limited Edition would be a suitable way of marking the first anniversary of the MX-5. Although this new version is mechanically the same as the standard car, it boasts an outstanding equipment list which we believe makes it a very special car. We will only ever market 250 and anticipate that each one will fast become a collectors item."

Following Mazda's success at Le Mans, Mazda UK launched its second limited edition model of the year.

The MX-5 Limited Edition.

An official publicity shot of the ultra rare MX-5 Le Mans.

73

Action from the third round of the 1991 Mazda MX-5 UK Cup. Robin Parsons (seen here leading the field into Druids) won the ten-lap event at Brands Hatch.

Writing for *MotorSport*, Simon Arron said: "In celebration of the company's first-ever Le Mans victory this year, Mazda has built a limited edition eyesore. Looking like a cross between a stick of Blackpool rock and a jar of Swarfega, the MX-5 Le Mans is equipped with a BBR turbo kit (boosting power to 150bhp) and body addenda. It does not come with a free respray voucher, but that doesn't appear to have dissuaded potential customers, as all 24 have now been sold at £20,499 apiece."

Obviously, Mr Arron wasn't too impressed with the colour scheme, which was essentially a facsimile of the bold design found on the winning Mazda – bright green, and even brighter orange, in a chequered pattern. At least two are known to have been resprayed black, whilst another was considerably toned down prior to sale.

The 1991 Earls Court Show saw the British debut of the MX-6. This elegant Grand Tourer (which eventually went on sale in the UK during February 1992) was joined on the Mazda stand by the recently launched MX-3 coupé (known in Japan as the Eunos Presso), the top version powered by the world's smallest V6 engine. The sporting theme was continued with the RX-7 Turbo Cabriolet and, of course, the MX-5, two of which were exhibited. Apart from the usual 121, 323 and 626 models, the display was completed by the Mazdaspeed 787B which had won at Le Mans earlier in the year, and the Group A 323 rally car that Hannu Mikkola had campaigned during the 1991 WRC season.

At the end of 1991, Mazda UK calculated it had sold 22,416 vehicles during the year. Although sales had fallen slightly compared to the previous year's figures, in actual fact, the MX-5 (accounting for 1986 units) had taken a larger percentage of Mazda's market share, increasing from 8.1 per cent to 8.8 per cent. The 1991 annual sales total was a record as far as Europe was concerned; including the UK figures, more than 14,000 MX-5s were sold during the year.

An English language brochure showing the MX-5 and RX-7 (the latter in closed coupé and Cabriolet forms). Although these are second generation RX-7s, the third generation was about to make its debut in Japan.

Italian advertising from the summer of 1991.

Vehicle identification numbers for US cars

The MX-5 has several variations for recording chassis numbers, but the VIN code on models shipped to the US is relatively straightforward, as well as being particularly useful. The 17-digit code is made up of a 'J' for Japan followed by 'M' for Mazda, and a '1' to signify a passenger car. The next two digits are 'N' and 'A,' which is to identify the NA (or M1) series within the MX-5 Miata run, and the '3' and '5' that come next represent a convertible body. An engine code follows, which is either a '1' or a '3.' The code JM1NA351xxxxxxxxx covers 1.6-litre machines, while JM1NA353xxxxxxxxx is for the later 1.8-litre cars. The ninth digit is a check digit, with a number between 0 and 9 (inclusive) or an 'X' being employed to fill the gap. Next up is a Model Year (MY) code, with 'L' for 1990, 'M' for 1991, 'N' for 1992, 'P' for 1993, 'R' for 1994, 'S' for 1995, 'T' for 1996, 'V' for 1997, and 'W' for 1998, which pops up on occasion. Next is a '0' for the Hiroshima plant, although quite a few NA1 cars have a '1' for the Hofu plant, which was used to keep up with the heavy demand created by the Mazda roadster in the early 1990s. The final six numbers cover the build number, reset at 100001 for each Model Year.

1992 Stateside

Changes for the 1992 model year had been announced in October 1991. Of course, the suspension modifications brought about in Japan during the summer of 1991 were inherited by the American cars, but more specifically for 1992, a remote bootlid release was fitted across the Miata range, and the Package B option now included an electric aerial; the optional hard-top (priced at $1500) at last came with a heated rear screen.

The base model had a $14,800 sticker price, with Package A adding $1370, and Package B putting $2040 on the invoice. Individual options included air conditioning (at $830), automatic transmission ($750),

ABS brakes ($900), a limited-slip differential ($250), CD player ($600), floormats ($65), and the aforementioned hard-top.

In March 1992, the Silver Stone Metallic body colour was discontinued and two new hues joined the line-up: Sunburst Yellow and Brilliant Black. The Sunburst Yellow shade was only available with the Package A upgrade, although air conditioning, an automatic gearbox, an lsd and a hard-top could be bought as options. Like the J Limited in Japan, which was finished in the same bright colour, production was restricted, and just 1500 cars were allocated for the States. As it happens, 1519 were sold in all, but these were to be both the first and last yellow

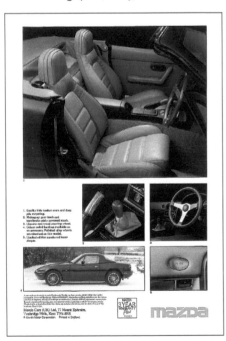

The sumptuous interior of the MX-5 Limited Edition, finished in tan leather. Only 250 of these models were built; each individually numbered.

American advertising for the 1992 model year Miata, seen here in postcard form.

NA models officially shipped to America, which attracted a $250 premium in the showroom.

The Brilliant Black model was not a limited edition, but had a higher specification than that of the run-of-the-mill Miata. Tan leather trim came as standard, and the hood was finished in the same colour to give a classy contrast with the coachwork. It came with alloy wheels, power steering, a radio/cassette unit, and electric windows included in the $17,050 price. For a further $1400, the black car could be specified with the newly-introduced Package C, including alloy wheels by BBS, a Nardi wooden gearknob, wooden handbrake trim, stainless treadplates, cruise control, an electric aerial, and headrest speakers. Over 7000 Brilliant Black Miatas were sold, prompting Mazda to rethink the Package C option for the 1993 season.

In March, *Road & Track* carried out a test comparing ten of the best handling cars available in America at that time. Of the Sunburst Yellow Miata (complete with yellow hard-top), racer Danny Sullivan said: "Well, it's a fun little car that's comfortable and easy to drive fast. The steering is responsive, but not too quick, and in the high speed corners the Miata feels very stable. Braking is very good; I was getting deeper and deeper into each corner and I never sensed any fade. It puts the power down well, and you'd get a slightly tail-out attitude on the fast stuff, but it was not bad overall. It's a little underpowered, but that's to be expected."

It was interesting comparing notes made by Roger Bell in the UK with those made by Danny Sullivan in the States, and reminded the author of a comment made by Maurice Ford, an old friend who used to race in the 1960s, regarding our mutual love of old Alfas. He observed that "You're never really going that fast, it just feels like you are!" The MX-5 had been cleverly engineered to feel the same way. Relatively narrow tyres (at least by modern sports car standards) combined with just enough power to excite, kept the limits low enough for people not to get into too much trouble; nothing will happen too quickly or suddenly as it might in a very high powered machine, or one with wider, grippier rubber. While someone like Bell or Sullivan could extract the best from the vehicle, it was designed to flatter any driver.

In a *Motor Trend* survey, an amazing 97.7 per cent of owners thought the fun-to-drive capabilities of the Miata were excellent; in fact, the car excelled in virtually every performance and creature comfort category, although it was perhaps significant that most bought the car initially on the grounds of styling. With 17 per cent saying they desired more power, handling was highlighted as a specific area that most owners liked and, with a fine reliability record, 73.6 per cent said they would be happy to buy another. All this press coverage and the various special editions helped keep sales at a high level, and allowed Mazda to divert some of its advertising budget to other vehicles in the range. Of the 52,712 MX-5s built in 1992 (which represents a figure 30 per cent higher than yearly expectations declared at the launch), no less than 24,964 of them found homes in the States.

Although rarely seen in IMSA events, the Miata could often be found competing in SCCA (Sports Car

The MX-5 SE of April 1992.

Club of America) meetings. Indeed, the Miata took SCCA Showroom Stock C honours for the first time in 1992, a category ideally suited to the little Mazda. On this occasion, it was Randy Pobst who took the victor's laurels, winning his heat by a fraction of a second!

The UK market in 1992

Features for the 1992 season included a remote bootlid release in the centre cubby box, security window etching, front number plate holders, and the use of a 'Finish Line 540' radio/cassette in place of the Clarion-badged unit. Standard colours included shades of red, white, blue and silver.

Following the success of the previous Limited Edition model, Mazda UK decided to offer the MX-5 Special Equipment. As the press release declared, it was "offered exclusively in black with a contrasting leather tan interior, together with a high specification list that includes anti-lock braking and an electric aerial. The MX-5 SE model goes on sale to the UK public on Monday 6 April and will be available throughout the Mazda Cars (UK) Ltd national dealer network priced at £17,788 (including car tax and VAT)."

Marketing Director, David Palmer, said: "The Mazda MX-5 has proved to be a universally popular car throughout the world. In the UK we have launched a series of special edition models to cater for people who want to own an MX-5 that is a little different from the rest. We believe that the Mazda MX-5 SE will be another success for us. It has all the attributes of the standard car coupled to a very extensive equipment list."

The Mazda MX-5 SE model was the first cosmetic upgrade to be offered in unlimited numbers in the British Isles, and featured Brilliant Black paintwork, tan leather seats and interior trim, a wood-rimmed steering wheel, wooden gearknob and handbrake handle, ABS braking, ten-spoke 7J x 15 polished alloys with locking wheelnuts, 'SE' badging (next to the MX-5 badge on the top left-hand side of the rear panel), chrome treadplates, an electric aerial, and an analogue clock. Interestingly, it was one of the first UK models to be built in the Hofu plant, although production would return to Hiroshima by the end of the year.

Whilst reviewing the MX-5 SE in its September 1992 issue, *MotorSport* also mentioned that Lotus had stopped building the new Elan: "Both received widespread press acclaim, but Japan's more cost-effective mass-production techniques have meant that the MX-5 is still being turned out – and sold – in high numbers, while the more expensive Lotus has recently been axed for financial reasons." Regarding the car itself, it was stated: "Designed as a convertible from the outset, the MX-5 is devoid of the rattles and body flex that often beset cabriolets that have been adapted from coupé originals. Build quality is first rate ... Whether or not one requires the SE pack is purely a question of taste and, perhaps, of budget. The bottom line is that the MX-5 remains a joy to drive, however you care to dress it up."

Mazda UK sold 1017 MX-5s in 1992. The total for the rest of Europe came to 5614 units during the same period, taking the figure to 6631 for the year.

Part of the MX-5 SE brochure showing salient points of the top model. Note the foglight below the rear bumper.

Time finally ran out for Mazda's other drophead – the RX-7 Cabriolet – leaving the MX-5 as the only convertible in the Hiroshima maker's line-up.

The S Special & S Limited

Although the recession which followed the boom of the late 1980s naturally hurt Japanese car manufacturers, it was a change in the local taxation laws and unfavourable exchange rates that did the real damage.

It was the exchange rates that were holding back Mazda; a luxury car division (called Amati) was planned to compete with the Lexus, Infiniti and Acura organisations but, in view of the economic situation, the idea was binned. Yoshihiro Wada, Mazda's President since December 1991, didn't seem overly worried in public, although it came as no surprise to followers of the industry that Ford's involvement with the company became more pronounced.

However, Mazda was determined to celebrate the third anniversary of the Eunos Roadster in style and, in July, announced the S Special. Production began in the following month so that it could take advantage of a scheduled minor change – side impact bars, and the option of an airbag (fitted in what for Japan was a unique four-spoke steering wheel, but basically the same as the one found in the States) – and sales started in September.

The S Special was a distinctly sporty version of the Eunos Roadster. Available in Classic Red or Brilliant Black, it came with manual transmission only, and was priced at 2,030,000 yen. It featured an uprated suspension with Bilstein shock absorbers, a front strut brace, 6J x 14 BBS alloy wheels fitted with 185/60 tyres, a Nardi three-spoke leather-trimmed steering wheel, Nardi leather gearknob, stainless treadplates and speaker grilles, and a rear spoiler. The only luxury item was the optional Mazda Sensory Sound System (a complicated Pioneer 130W stereo system that included a CD player), which was priced at 220,000 yen.

In December 1992, Mazda announced the S Limited – a run of 1000 cars based on the S Special. Sales began in January 1993 (the first car was chassis NA6CE-209203), with the price set at 2,350,000 yen. Finished in Brilliant Black, the model came with a red leather interior, attractive gold-coloured BBS alloys, and the aforementioned Sensory Sound System.

All told, 18,657 Eunos Roadsters were sold in Japan during 1992, almost three times as many as were sold in the whole of Europe. Incidentally, the 250,000th MX-5 (built at the Hiroshima plant on 9 November 1992) went to

The M2-1001

The M2 project was established in November 1990, with the M2-1001 the first offering. All of the staff involved (about 30 people) were Mazda workers, and included Masakatsu Kato (the man behind numerous Mazda concept cars), Hirotaka Tachibana (the development engineer who had been of great importance on the first generation MX-5 project) and Masanori Mizuochi, now Chairman of the Roadster Club of Japan (RCOJ). The main objective of the project was to be a direct contact between the company and the car's users, as well as building MX-5 specials for show purposes and test marketing.

The M2-1001 was announced on 1 December 1991 (by which time the M2 team had settled down in its new headquarters in Setagaya, Tokyo), but delivery didn't start until March 1992. The car featured a 130bhp engine (with a 10.7:1 c/r, lightened flywheel, and modified ECU and exhaust) linked to a five-speed manual transmission, a stiffened chassis, modified suspension, and wider 195/50 tyres mounted on 15-inch, eight-spoke alloy wheels. Finished in dark blue paint, and with a rollbar as standard, the whole package weighed in at 960kg (2112lb).

From the outset, it was stated that only 300 were being built, and this fact contributed greatly to tempting buyers to part with a hefty 3,400,000 yen. For this kind of money, it was possible to buy a basic Nissan 300ZX, or a high spec Toyota Supra in Japan. Nevertheless, the M2-1001 was heavily over-subscribed. In the end, a lottery system was used to determine who would get one, resulting in many disappointed enthusiasts; Mazda could quite easily have sold at least 600 more!

The M2-1001 was the first product to be developed by the M2 organisation, Tachibana's brainchild, established in November 1990. Announced in December 1991, the 1001 was obviously more muscular around the front end, but there were also a number of delightful touches, such as the racing-style alloy fuel filler cap and door mirrors. Cars were numbered from 001 to 300.

Interior of the M2-1001 – Tachibana's favourite M2 vehicle, sometimes referred to as the 'Clubman' model.

Australia, and is now an exhibit at the Australian National Motor Museum.

The US market for 1993

For 1993, the car's suspension was refined to give "improved ride qualities without sacrificing handling," but the thing that most noticed was the new badge on the nose (leading to the deletion of the 'Mazda' decal on the front bumper – even though some retouched catalogue pictures left them on!) and the centre caps on the alloy wheel option. In addition, the steering wheel boss now had 'SRS Airbag' in place of the previous 'Mazda' script.

An AM/FM stereo radio/cassette with integral digital clock became standard on all cars, having previously been part of the Package A option, and Brilliant Black was added as a regular colour; the base Miata was now priced at $15,300.

The option packages were rearranged for the 1993 model year and included the following items: Option Package A ($1300) added power-assisted steering, a leather-wrapped steering wheel, electrically-adjustable mirrors, alloy wheels and headrest speakers to the basic model. Package B ($2000) included everything in Package A, plus cruise control, electric windows, and an automatic electric aerial. The new Package C ($2700) had all the items in Package B, plus a tan-coloured interior with leather seat facings, and a tan vinyl top. This was available on all paintwork options with the exception of cars finished in Mariner Blue, which could be supplied with the standard black trim only.

Mazda's Sensory Sound System (MSSS) could be bought as a separate option, as could ABS braking (with Package B or C), automatic transmission, a limited-slip differential (for manual cars), a hard-top, and air conditioning.

Midway through the year, the Miata Limited Edition made its entrance. The American cousin of the S Limited, it was finished in Brilliant Black with a red leather interior (a red vinyl tonneau cover was also included), and came with the usual luxury touches – air conditioning, a leather-trimmed

The S Special of September 1992 vintage, seen here in both colour finishes available on this sporty model. The car nearest the camera is fitted with the Sensory Sound System.

In December 1992, Mazda announced the S Limited. Finished in Brilliant Black, it came with a red leather interior, attractive gold-coloured BBS alloys, and the Sensory Sound System.

Rear three-quarter view of the S Limited – a run of 1000 cars based on the S Special.

Interior of the S Limited.

steering wheel, a Nardi leather gearknob, cruise control, the MSSS stereo system, power windows and mirrors, stainless treadplates and speaker grilles, red floormats, a special keyfob, and even a Miata book. However, power-assisted steering, ABS, a limited-slip differential, 14-inch BBS alloy wheels fitted with 185/60 tyres, an uprated suspension with Bilstein shock absorbers, and front and rear spoilers (along with a lowered rear valance to match) were also included in the $22,000 list price. Only 1500 examples were ever built but, as *Sports Car International* pointed out, with the horsepower output unchanged, "the engine is not enough to warrant such a harsh suspension."

The Miata was the SCCA Showroom Stock C class winner again (this time courtesy of Michael Galati, in a race dominated by the little roadsters), although it wasn't the only car in the Mazda range to acquire an important title, as the

new RX-7 received the 1993 'Import Car of the Year' award from *Motor Trend* magazine.

Sales in America were still falling, but 21,588 units was a more than respectable figure for the year; across the border, Canada took another 1501 (Canadian sales had been falling steadily by around 25 per cent year-on-year since their peak in 1990). Added together, this accounted

The Miata seen competing in SCCA racing, where it soon acquired an excellent reputation. It took the Showroom Stock C title on several occasions.

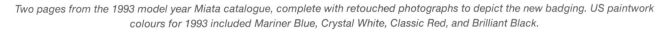

Two pages from the 1993 model year Miata catalogue, complete with retouched photographs to depict the new badging. US paintwork colours for 1993 included Mariner Blue, Crystal White, Classic Red, and Brilliant Black.

The MX-5 and alternative fuels

Development of the electric MX-5 had started in January 1992 and was scheduled to continue for two years. The project was set up with the objective of exploring alternative fuels, as environmental concerns were paramount in virtually every country around the world, not least in Japan, which has had quite a strict policy since the 1970s.

In February 1993, Mazda UK released the following statement: "Still very much a prototype project, as only three have been built, the battery powered Mazda MX-5 was designed in conjunction with the Chugoku Electric Power Company and will be used by the company to run practicality tests for using electric cars on a daily basis.

"In testing, the electric Mazda MX-5 has achieved performance figures compatible with a petrol driven 1.5-litre automatic. Powered by an electric AC motor, the energy source is taken from 16 nickel cadmium batteries situated in the engine bay. With a top speed of 80mph [128kph], acceleration of 0-25mph [40kph] in just 4.2 seconds and a range of up to 111 miles [178km], an electrically powered MX-5 is being considered as a viable alternative for the future."

Weight was the biggest problem. With power-assisted steering and air conditioning, the electric MX-5 weighed in at a hefty 1410kg (3102lb) in an unladen state. This was due to the four batteries up front and another 12 in the boot. In reality, only lighter, more compact batteries would ever make electric power a viable option in a car of this type.

Hydrogen power deserved more careful consideration. It emits no hydrocarbons or carbon dioxide when it burns; it has high potential energy, and can be used in all types of engines.

In Japan, the Ministry of International Trade & Industry (MITI) was aiming to use hydrogen to gradually replace other energy sources. Mazda was called in to help with the project and conducted a year-long monitoring test in conjunction with the Nippon Steel Corporation's Hirohata works located near Kobe. R&D head, Seiji Tanaka, said: "Our first objective is to use available fuels more efficiently by producing better engines. At present we are researching the Miller-cycle and developing lean-burn technology. Our second objective is to investigate alternative fuels such as natural gas and methanol and electric cars. But this will not cut pollution. Hydrogen offers many advantages over all these, especially electric cars, and with the rotary engine fuelled by hydrogen, performance is very close to the petrol engine."

The hydrogen was stored in metal hydride powder, made up predominantly of titanium and iron. When the gas is cooled under pressure, the powder will absorb the atoms, allowing safe storage of a litre of gas in just one cubic centimetre of powder. Heating the powder releases the gas. The only problem with this method is that the boot is filled with aluminium canisters.

The hydrogen powered car had a rotary engine from the normally aspirated RX-7, but externally (apart from the obvious script down the sides of the vehicles), there was nothing to tell it apart from an MX-5 straight out of the showroom. It was the same story inside, the only exception being a more appropriate fuel gauge.

The electric car also looked surprisingly standard. Again, the fuel gauge was replaced, this time with a charge meter. The electric MX-5 was very quiet but, as noted earlier, not particularly quick. In fact, 0-62mph (100kph) took 21.5 seconds – a figure that doesn't really stack up against 9.4 seconds for a petrol driven machine. The hydrogen model, however, could cover the same yardstick in just 13.0 seconds, which is much more acceptable. It could also reach 93mph (149kph) with a five-speed manual transmission, but we shall have to wait and see whether or not hydrogen power has a future.

One of three electric MX-5s built to test the potential of alternative fuels. Mazda also built a hydrogen-powered version, which proved the more practical of the two in everyday situations. However, in early 1995, the M2 organisation offered a course giving guidance on how to convert an MX-5 to electric power.

for the bulk of exports during 1993, as European sales fell to an all-time low.

The 1993 model year in Britain

The Mazda stand at the 1992 British Motor Show (held at the NEC between 24 October and 1 November), had the new RX-7 as its star attraction. As the press release stated: "One of the highlights of the stand will be the Mazda RX-7 Turbo. This stunning new sports [model] created a sensation at its international debut in Tokyo at the end of 1991. The RX-7 has just gone on sale in the UK, but with just 120 cars available this year, it is set to be a very exclusive sports car." Known in Japan as the Anfini RX-7 (and sold through the Anfini sales channel, established in 1991), the 237bhp machine was capable of covering 0-60 in just 5.3 seconds, before powering on towards a top speed of 150mph (240kph).

The RX-7 joined a distinctly sporting line-up, including the MX-3, MX-5 and MX-6, as well as the 323, 626, and luxury Xedos 6 range. To reinforce Mazda's desired sporty image, the 323F used by Patrick Watts in the 1992 British Touring Car Championship was also on display.

From 4 January 1993, a number of Mazdas were subjected to price increases. The Mazda MX-3 1.8i now cost £15,729, the standard MX-5 was £15,780, while the MX-6 started at £18,519. However, the recently launched RX-7 remained at £32,536.

On 5 May, Mazda UK announced the second MX-5 SE. This latest MX-5 SE was basically the same as the original, although the alloy wheels were different on this edition (6.5J x 15), and the stereo unit was also changed. The press release noted: "A new 1993 special version of the Mazda MX-5 will go on sale on Tuesday 1 June, available only in Brilliant Black with an extensive standard equipment list.

"The Mazda MX-5 SE, priced at £18,686, is offered in black and comes with contrasting tan leather interior with extensive use of wooden mahogany trim. The specification

The hydrogen-powered MX5.

The MX-5 SE of May 1993.

A 1993 MX-5 in standard UK trim, just before European models adopted the new corporate badge on the nose panel and wheel centres.

Patrick Watts with the Xedos 6 developed by RD Motorsport for the 1993 BTCC season. Watts, who won the 1990 Mazda MX-5 UK Cup, had driven a two-litre 323F in the previous year, but with little success. David Leslie drove the Xedos 6 in 1994, but Mazda finished the season early, pulling out of the series in July.

Some of the cars on display at the 1992 Motor Show held at the NEC on the outskirts of Birmingham. Nearest the camera and to the left is the Xedos 6, while the new, third generation RX-7 can be seen next to it. A 626 is behind the RX-7, with the elegant MX-6 making up the foursome.

list is impressive and includes an anti-lock braking system, electrical aerial, and seven-spoke chrome-plated alloy wheels."

Jan Smith, the new Marketing Director of Mazda UK, said: "The Mazda MX-5 has proved to be one of the most successful and sought-after cars currently available. The fact that production worldwide has now exceeded 250,000 speaks volumes for the popularity and attraction of the car ... The 1993 Mazda MX-5 SE owners can be sure that they will be driving a very exclusive car indeed."

By July, a number of changes had begun to filter through for the next season. An electric aerial was declared standard, as was the Clarion CRX52 radio/cassette unit, whilst, on the safety front, the MX-5 now came with side-impact door protection beams. The new corporate chrome badge appeared on the nose as well, replacing the old 'Mazda' decal applied to the lower left-hand side of the bumper (a handy identifying feature when trying to date vehicles).

During 1993, Mazda UK sold a total of 18,944 vehicles, but only 910 of these were MX-5s – less than 5 per cent of Mazda's market share in the British Isles. MX-5 sales for the rest of Europe added up to 3914 units for the year.

News from the Antipodes

After a high of 1446 sales in 1990, the Australian market was becoming something of a disappointment; only 746 sales were recorded in 1991, and 1992's figures fell again to just 502 units. The press was still behind the car, but, ultimately, it was the public that had to buy it. In an attempt to try and make the convertible more tempting, Mazda launched the $39,990 MX-5 Classic.

Finished in red with a tan leather interior, the package included BBS alloys, a CD player, a Nardi gearknob with matching handbrake trim, and even a signed picture of Toshihiko Hirai (he left the company shortly after to become a university lecturer).

Limited to 100 units (this was Australia's fourth limited edition, incidentally – the first was a Neo Green model launched at the end of 1990 and restricted to 300 examples; there were 55 produced in Malibu Gold during 1992, and another 300 in Neo Green later that year), it sold out almost immediately, despite competition from the vastly improved Ford Capri, which was built in Australia, and was some $11,000 cheaper. However, including the Classic, total Australian sales for 1993 still amounted to only 453 cars.

Dashboard of the French 1993 model year MX-5. Most pictures used in catalogues were the same across Europe (including the UK), and were simply reversed and retouched as necessary for left- and right-hand drive cars; only the dashboard shots had to be specially taken. For the 1995 model year worldwide, the traditional-style calibrations on the oil pressure gauge were replaced by 'idiot-proof' 'L' and 'H' markings at each extremity.

Italian advertising from the summer of 1993, this piece showing the entire Mazda range for the European market.

A page from the Australian catalogue of February 1992, describing the MX-5 as "The Reincarnation of the Classic Sports Car."

Rear view of the model for the Australian market. Sales were strong in the Antipodes during 1989 and 1990, but dropped off rapidly thereafter.

Interior of the Australian specification car. The handbrake remained in this position on all cars for all markets, regardless of whether they were left- or right-hand drive.

The B6-ZE (RS) engine. It should be noted that, on this 1.6-litre unit, the maker's name and 'DOHC 16-VALVE' is cast into the metal: soon these would become a useful identifying feature.

M2-1002

After the phenomenal success of the M2-1001, you'd be forgiven for believing that the 1002 couldn't fail. It was a similar scenario: 300 cars would be built – again, finished in dark blue, but with a tan hood. The 1.6-litre engine was left as standard on this occasion (with a five-speed gearbox), as were the chassis details.

While special wheels and a subtle chin spoiler were employed, it was the cockpit that was the main feature on the 1002. Wood trim came from Yamaha, and ivory leather was used almost everywhere. Even the top roll on the fascia was leather, but this time in a dark blue. Without a doubt, the interior was truly beautiful, and would have made any Italian coachbuilder proud. All this added an extra 10kg (22lb) to the weight of its predecessor, despite the lack of power steering (something which 1001 had).

Announced at the end of 1992, delivery started in February 1993. However, by the end of May when it was discontinued, only 100 of the 3,000,000 yen machines had been sold; some of the interior parts were later used on the Tokyo Limited of late 1993. The failure of 1002 was almost certainly down to a question of timing. It's relevant to remember that the MX-5 was launched at the height of an economic boom when people – especially in Japan – had plenty of money to spare for luxury items. The 1001 seemed to catch the mood of the moment; by the time the 1002 was launched, the economy had slowed down somewhat ... the bubble had burst. It is hard to imagine Japan struggling but, by all accounts, people were selling cars rather than buying them during this period, and this goes a long way towards explaining the 1002's disappointing sales.

M2-1003 also concentrated on interior appointments (it also had a Rod Millen rear deck aero cover and BBS alloys), but, after the poor response to 1002, the project was shelved before seeing the light of day.

Sadly, the M2-1002 (seen in the foreground in this shot) was not as successful as the 1001, pictured in the background. All M2 cars had unique tail badges and a numbered plate by the nearside door mirror. M2 numbers ran consecutively, so the 1002 series was ultimately allocated 301 to 400.

Another view of the M2-1002, with, above, a close-up of its stylish interior.

Chapter 5

THE NA2
AND SWAN SONG

Kenichi Yamamoto, one of the main supporters of the LWS project, retired in the early part of 1993. Voted RJC 'Man of the Year' in 1991 (the RX-7 was voted RJC 'Car of the Year' at the same time, incidentally), he had witnessed enormous changes within Mazda and could be justifiably proud of the role he had played in the company's development.

Things were happening on the Eunos Roadster front as well. In February 1993, the V Special adopted the Sensory Sound System as standard but, more importantly, in July, Mazda announced the first major face-lift of the MX-5 – the so-called NA2 version. With Hirai declaring his wish to leave the company (he finally left in March 1993), Shiro Yoshioka was put in charge of the project.

Complying with forthcoming regulation changes meant a sizeable weight gain for the 1994 season car. Mazda concluded that the only way to keep the vehicle's performance at its current level was to increase engine capacity. Initial thoughts were to retain the 1.6-litre four and introduce a new two-litre unit to augment it. Instead, the 1.8-litre BP-type engine from the Familia GT was chosen, largely because it was a good compromise: some of the Roadster's edge on economy would have been lost with a two-litre lump (and meant higher insurance, too), while the 1.6 would have struggled to remain sporty with the heavier body, especially when combined with an automatic transmission. Modified to give 130bhp at 6500rpm, the 1839cc unit was given the BP-ZE designation.

The body was strengthened in anticipation of the new engine, with 'performance rods' added up front and in a U-shaped configuration at the back. In addition, a cockpit brace bar was introduced, joining the seatbelt anchor towers, and working in tandem with side-impact bars to further enhance rigidity and safety

The suspension settings were revised to suit, while the brake discs increased in diameter from 235mm (9.2in) to 255mm (10.0in) at the front, and from 231mm (9.1in) to 251mm (9.9in) at the rear. A Torsen limited-slip differential came with the five-speed cars (earlier models had a viscous LSD), and the optional alloy wheels were completely restyled. Interestingly, despite the rim width increasing to 6J (from 5.5J), each wheel was around 1kg (2lb) lighter than the original design, representing quite a saving overall.

Although the manual gearbox ratios were untouched, the final-drive ratio was changed from 4.3:1 to 4.1:1. The optional four-speed automatic transmission was now an electronically controlled unit with slightly different ratios, but the final-drive was actually the same as the manual cars at 4.1:1 (instead of 4.444:1 as used on the 1.6-litre automatics), signifying another important change.

The 1.6-litre cars had carried the NA6CE chassis designation, whereas the new 1.8-litre models were given the NA8C code (production began in August on chassis NA8C-100016). A useful identifying feature at the rear of the car was the 'Roadster' badge, the script now red

それは、バランスの探究。

ユーノスロードスターならではの「人馬一体感」。その楽しさに満ちた世界が、いまあらたな進化を遂げた。目指したのは、運動性、安全性、快適性など、これからのライトウェイトスポーツが問うべき、すべての能力の高次元バランス。DOHCエンジンの排気量アップ、ボディとサスペンションの剛性アップ、さらに、ブレーキ性能のアップとオートマチックのリニューアル…。すべては、ライトウェイトスポーツ本来の人馬一体感と、すぐれた危険回避能力に代表される安全性、そして、日常的な扱いやすさを同時に進化させるための施策である。新しいロードスターに託した開発陣の思い。それは、ステアリングを一度でも握れば、たちどころに知ることができる。

ユーノスロードスターは、あらたに自然吸気1800DOHCエンジンを搭載した。最高出力130ps/6500rpm（ネット*1）、最大トルク16.0kg-m/4500rpm。高速タイプのバルブタイミング、軽量コンロッド、新たに採用したホットワイヤー式のエアフロメーターをはじめとする吸気抵抗の軽減などにより、レッドゾーンまで一気に吹き上がる高回転特性とともに、ぶ厚い低中速トルクを確保。また、ドライバーの意志にリニアに応えるアクセルレスポンスをさらに研ぎ澄ました。5段マニュアルトランスミッションには、確実で滑らかなギアシフトをサポートするため、セカンド・ギアにダブルコーンシンクロを採用した。主制御用の電子制御式4段オートマチック［C-AT］*2は、よりスムーズな走行フィールを実現。パワーとノーマルモードを自動的に切り替えるオートパワー制御も備える。また、1/2/3速を任意に固定できるホールドモード」や、ダイレクト＆シャープな走りを実現する。そして、トランスミッションとデフをリジッドに結合するアルミ製P.P.F.（パワー・プラント・フレーム）、エンジンルクのダイレクトな低速走行とシフトフィールの高剛性感を実現する。FRのユーノスロードスターならではのアイテム、5段マニュアル車にはレスポンスにすぐれたトルク感応拡張型リミテッドスリップ“トルセン”LSD*3（Torque Sensing Limited Slip Differencial）を装備。オイルの粘性を利用して差動を制御するビスカスLSDに対して、両輪のトルク差を感応しながら適切なトルク配分を行なうことで安定したトラクションがよりダイレクトに得られる。これにより、アクセルワークで車体姿勢を積極的にコントロールすることも可能にしている。排気システムは、排気マニホールドからテールパイプに至るまですべてステンレスパイプ製、高周波音をカットし、抜けがよく低音のきいたエグゾーストサウンドとしている。

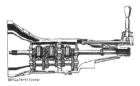

1800DOHCの冴え。

A double-page spread from the Japanese catalogue of August 1993 showing the new 1.8-litre engine (note the raised details on the cam covers), the Torsen differential, and electronically-controlled automatic transmission. Not shown, but important nonetheless, is the larger fuel tank fitted to NA2 models, with its capacity upped to 48 litres (10.6 Imperial gallons, or 12.7 US).

The new 1800 series in all its glory. Again, the Japanese market range was very extensive.

instead of the original black. Other distinguishing features included a different number plate holder, standard rear mudflaps, and the addition of large elasticated door pockets at the cost of armrests. On the base models, Classic Red, Silver Stone Metallic and Chaste White became the extent of the standard colour range, signifying the end of Crystal White and Mariner Blue.

Announced in July, sales of the 1.8 range started in September. At 1,791,000 yen, the manual only 1.8-litre Series I standard model served as an entry level Eunos Roadster, but the Special Package version (available with either manual or automatic transmission) again made up the bulk of sales. Weighing in at 990kg (2178lb) in manual form (10kg, or 22lb, more than the basic car), it was priced at 1,966,000 yen, whilst the automatic gearbox added 30kg (66lb) and 50,000 yen.

The V Special was continued (2,336,000 yen in manual form, or 2,386,000 yen with an automatic gearbox), but there was now also the V Special Type II. The extra 100,000 yen needed to secure one added a highly polished finish to the seven-spoke alloy wheels, chrome door mirrors, and a tan coloured soft-top.

The line-up was completed by the manual only S Special, priced at 2,111,000 yen. Based on the Special Package model, it came in either Laguna Blue Metallic or Brilliant Black, and featured an array of tempting items: an uprated suspension with Bilstein shocks and thicker anti-roll bars, a front tower brace, rear body brace, 14-inch BBS alloy wheels, polished treadplates and kickplates (which surrounded the door speakers), and a Nardi steering wheel. Incidentally, prices were around 36,000 yen less in Tokyo due to lower delivery charges.

The V Special II made its debut with the announcement of the 1800 series.

Interior of the late 1993 V Special.

The 1.8-litre Special Package model, seen here finished in Classic Red.

Interior of the latest Eunos Roadster (this is a Special Package model), clearly showing the Momo steering wheel and the cockpit brace bar fitted behind the seats. The base cars had a vaguely similar three-spoke wheel, but made in-house.

A few months later, in November, Mazda released a limited edition of just 40 cars finished in Brilliant Black with a tan hood. Known as the Tokyo Limited, this employed a number of interior parts used from the M2-1002 run. The cream leather trim was beautiful, and the added detailing fully justified the 2,458,000 yen price tag – even the automatic version, at 2,508,000 yen, seemed cheap compared with the 3,000,000 asked for the M2-1002.

In December, according to the *Mazda Yearbook*, "Mazda and Ford entered into a long-term strategic relationship to enhance their competitive strength" and, in the same month, another limited edition Eunos Roadster was announced – the J Limited II. Based on the Special Package model, the J Limited II was finished in Sunburst Yellow, just like the original J Limited. However, the windscreen surround was finished in black on this occasion. Bucket seats with independent headrests were used, a CD player was a standard fitment, and Pirelli P700-Z tyres were mounted on the familiar 6J x 14 seven-spoke alloys. Limited to just 800 examples, prices started at 2,030,000 yen for the five-speed version, with the optional automatic transmission adding a further 50,000 yen. Roadster sales in Japan added up to a total of 16,789 units for the year, by the way.

An M2 finale

Despite the lack of a new model, the M2 team had been keeping itself busy since the debut of the M2-1002. In addition to the 1003, many interesting projects had been carried out on various Mazda vehicles, but none were thought suitable for production for one reason or another. In the process, two particularly stunning Eunos Roadster-based machines were unfortunately allowed to slip through the net – M2-1006 and M2-1008.

M2-1006 came about in mid-1992, and featured wider bodywork, RX-7 suspension pieces and a 220bhp three-litre V6 engine from the Sentia (929). Naturally, with this much power, it was quite a handful. To keep the car in check, 225/50 VR16 tyres were fitted at the front, with 245/50s at the back.

Ironically, the car was not in keeping with Tachibana's image, which was to make something along the lines of the Dodge Viper. It was simply not as exciting to drive as he'd hoped, and the project was ended there and then.

The M2-1008 was an attractive coupé, with a Club Racer-type nose (complete with faired-in headlights) and a tail styled along the lines of the Ferrari Daytona – even the round rear lights seemed to pay tribute to the Pininfarina design, although single lamps were used on the Mazda instead of two on each side, as on the Italian car.

Before closing down the M2 operation in April 1995 ("due to the faltering business situation within Mazda itself"), the team managed to get a third and final Eunos Roadster-based car into production – the M2-1028. Announced in February 1994 at a price of 2,800,000 yen (delivery began in March), the 1028 was based on the five-speed, 1.8-litre model, but had a stronger – yet lighter – body (helped by a front strut brace and an aluminium roll-over bar) and a highly tuned engine.

Tipping the scales at 960kg (2112lb), it had 30 per cent better torsional rigidity; in fact, it was easily as strong as most closed cars. This, in addition to newly developed Bridgestone tyres and a harder suspension set-up, allowed an impressive improvement in handling (0.93g has been measured on the skidpan).

The 1028 was available in either Dark Blue or Chaste White, although a hood was not supplied – at the end of the day, the car was intended to be more at home on the track than commuting to work on a daily basis! However, a lightweight custom hard-top was part of the package. Of the 300 built, 185 were sold in white (the most popular colour for cars in Japan), leaving 115 finished in the blue shade. At least the M2 project went out on a high note, as the M2-1028 sold out within a couple of months.

There was one final Miata project – the M2-1031 – that allowed wheelchair users the opportunity to enjoy MX-5 Roadster motoring. Sadly, time ran out for the people at M2, and the project was not allowed to progress.

The M2-1028 finished in Chaste White and Dark Blue – the two shades available on this model. As well as a number of modifications to make the bodyshell stronger, the 1028 had an aluminium bootlid, lighter wheels, and glassfibre seats to save weight. The engine featured a higher compression ratio, lightened flywheel, tuned ECU, and a free-flow exhaust system. With 140bhp on tap, this was the most powerful M2 engine released to the public. M2-1028 numbers ran from 401 to 700.

The wacky M2-1006, which Quattroroute described as "La Miata di Batman," pictured at the M2 headquarters in Tokyo's Setagaya. The M2 building was quite a landmark, and was even featured in magazines like Elle Deco.

M2 Inc advertising from mid-1993, featuring the M2-1008 coupé.

Another view of the Special Package model, this time with the optional hard-top in place.

The S Special at speed in an ideal sports car arena.

1994 model year in the UK

Although the SE continued to be listed at £18,686 (its original launch price), by now the cost of a standard 1.6i model had risen to a hefty £16,490. However, on 18 April, Mazda UK announced two new models to supercede them – the MX-5 1.8i and 1.8iS.

The main difference compared with earlier models was obviously the increase in engine size (to 1839cc), raising power from a modest 114bhp to 130bhp, and boosting maximum torque output to 112lbft. However, the new models also benefited from an uprated suspension and a stiffer body (through the use of the additional bracing described earlier) to give a better ride and improve handling. Inside, the old high backed seats were replaced with a new type (like those found on the J Limited II) incorporating an adjustable headrest. At the same time,

door armrests were deleted, with door pockets taking their place.

The top 1.8iS model had all the previous 1.6i features, but added ABS, a driver's side airbag, new (and lighter) 6J x 14 seven-spoke alloy wheels, a rheostat for the panel lights, electric mirrors, an electric aerial, and a Clarion CRX87R detachable radio/cassette unit.

The 1.8i was the basic model, coming with 5.5J x 14 steel wheels, a urethane steering wheel, and a generally lower level of equipment. The base model was sold without power-assisted steering, the ABS system, airbag, electric windows, internal bootlid release, and radio/cassette unit. However, to keep insurance companies happy, both models were fitted with an immobiliser as standard.

Going on sale from 2 May, Laguna Blue Metallic and Chaste White replaced the Mariner Blue and Crystal White shades, whilst British Racing Green and Brilliant Black

The options available for the Eunos Roadster. Many of these items eventually found their way onto Japan's various limited edition models.

The J Limited II with its distinctive Sunburst Yellow coachwork. The wheels – the latest seven-spoke design – were obviously different to those of the original J Limited, but the black windscreen surround was another useful distinguishing feature.

Interior of the J Limited II.

became available as standard colour options. Classic Red and Silver Stone Metallic made up the six-colour range.

Complete Car tested a basic 1.8i in its August 1994 issue, and gave the Design & Quality, Going & Stopping, Handling & Grip and Value & Economy categories four out of five stars each, with only Comfort & Equipment falling behind with three stars. After outlining the key points in the

development of the LWS model, the magazine continued: "As the years rolled by, a few changes began to detract from the concept. First, the car started to creep upmarket in trim levels and price. Then there was the compulsory catalytic converter, which robbed the engine of much of its pep.

"Mazda has corrected both these faults in the latest revision. The car now comes in two guises, with a cheaper, stripped-down version, tested here, for people who want to get back to basics. Unlike the pricier 1.8iS, the 1.8i has no power steering, no anti-lock brakes, no airbag, manual windows, steel wheels rather than alloys, and a plastic rather than leather steering wheel. But at £14,495, it's £2900 cheaper than the iS and around £2000 cheaper than the old 1.6.

"The engine has a low speed urge that was never present on the 1.6, but it still has the rorty exhaust note that the company worked hard to achieve with the original car. It has perhaps lost a little of its smoothness at high revs, but it performs well – and smoothness is not the ultimate aim in this sort of machine. The gearbox still works with beautiful click-click precision and tiny movements ... The new MX-5 also has substantially better roadholding than the old model, particularly at the rear. The handling is better, too."

Despite little change in the overall power-to-weight ratio, the now defunct monthly recorded a 0-60 time of 8.6 seconds, and a top speed of 119mph (190kph).

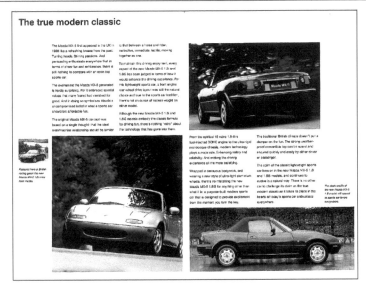

The true modern classic

The opening pages of the first British catalogue to feature the 1.8-litre models. A nose badge was added at this time.

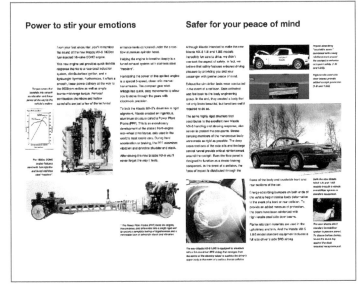

Power to stir your emotions   **Safer for your peace of mind**

Another spread from the British catalogue, highlighting the improvements, not only in power (for the 1.8-litre machine) but safety as well. The PPF was retained on the new series.

During the test, 29.3mpg was returned overall, with 40.9mpg being possible at a steady 56mph (90kph).

In the same month, *MotorSport* tried the 1.8iS. It was noted: "Until this spring, such changes as there had been were more cosmetic than technical. Now, however, the original 1.6 engine (which was actually quite perky, though made to sound more so by a trick exhaust) has been superseded by a 1.8 unit derived from that in the 323, albeit lightened. Power has accordingly risen 15 per cent, to 130bhp – on a par with the MX-5 UK Cup racers that provided the basis for a one-make series in 1990/91. The car is heavier, though (by 50 or

70kg [110lb or 154lb], according to which model you choose), and doesn't feel substantially nippier. Indeed, top speed is little changed, at a claimed 123mph [197kph] (up from 121), and 0-62mph [0-100kph] will take an estimated 8.6 seconds (another fractional gain).

"In parallel with engine development, the chassis has also been modified. Although the original was a paragon of balance, and torsional rigidity, further bracing has been added, and the suspension has been tuned to cope with the extra weight. Mazda says that its intention was to 'suppress roll during the initial stages of cornering and improve the overall ride comfort while maximising the handling.'"

In September, *Complete Car* published a comparison test. After the results came in, the MX-5 1.8i was declared "the best all-rounder. This will suit the sports car enthusiast just as much as the image-conscious looking for a fashion statement. It looks great and chic but is extremely enjoyable to drive, and still offers traditionally excellent Mazda build quality and generous warranty into the bargain. In this cheaper, stripped-down version, it is actually a pleasant change to find features such as manual window winders and steel wheels. This is the car which, at a push, could most easily be used as an only car."

The £14,495 Mazda was awarded eight out of ten points, while the £16,600 Caterham 7 K-series took seven points. The Suzuki Cappuccino, the cheapest of the bunch at just over £12,000, got six, the same as the Reliant Scimitar Sabre, which was slightly cheaper than the MX-5 at £13,995.

At the end of 1994, Mazda UK calculated that a total of 18,047 vehicles had been sold, 1250 of which were MX-5s – the rest of Europe only achieved 3769 sales during the same period. This was naturally a vast improvement on the previous year, but how long could it last?

Australian update

Interestingly, the December 1994 issue of the Australian *Wheels* magazine, which looked back on the staff's favourite cars of the year, said: "How do you explain other manufacturers' reluctance to tackle the MX-5? [It] still holds the monopoly on user-friendly, two-seater sports cars – a fact weighing ever more heavily in its $40K price tag."

In Australia, although it was a fraction more expensive than the Honda CRX, the MX-5 was cheaper than a Toyota MR2 and about the same as a front-wheel drive Celica. Australia had two 1.8-litre models – the standard MX-5 1.8 and the Clubman, with its Bilstein shocks, uprated anti-roll bars, LSD, PAS deleted, and special badging. But

A 1994 model year Miata in White. America listed Classic Red, Laguna Blue Metallic, White, and Brilliant Black for 1994; the tan leather trim that came with the Package C option was available on all four colours.

the competition, armed with convertibles from various corners of Europe, was preparing to muscle in on some of the Mazda's action.

Australian sales for 1994 amounted to 404 units, but dropped to just 196 in the following year.

America in 1994 and 1995

Of course, the biggest change for the 1994 model year (announced in October 1993), was adoption of the 1.8-litre engine. In US guise, the power output was listed at 128bhp at 6500rpm (a gain of 12bhp), with maximum torque quoted at 110lbft. Not only was this an increase of 10lbft, it was also more useable, coming in 500rpm lower down the rev range than before.

The American market naturally gained all the body modifications associated with the 1.8-litre machine (namely performance rods front and rear, and a vinyl-covered brace bar connecting the seatbelt anchor towers), as well as the Torsen differential and restyled alloys (both in the Package A option), uprated suspension and larger brakes, all introduced with the bigger engined Eunos Roadster in Japan. In addition, for the US, dual airbags were made a standard fitment.

Mariner Blue was replaced by the new Laguna Blue Metallic shade, there was a fresh white hue known simply as White in the States, and the 'Miata' script on the rear badge was now in red instead of black. At the start of the 1994 model year, the Miata's base price was just $16,450 but, in reality, few cars were sold without one of the option packages. The popular Package A, priced at $1710, included power steering, alloy wheels, a leather-

While the covers on the 1992 and 1993 issues had not been the most exciting ever, the cover of the 1994 model year Miata brochure was particularly attractive. The little Mazda entered the Guinness Book of Records in 1994 when the Miata Club of America managed to get 242 cars running together at Indianapolis.

A

First, the Mazda Miata burned up the track to become the SCCA Showroom Stock C Champion.

roadster

Now it's ready to burn up the road. Presenting the new Miata R Package. A lightweight racer with

so racy we

128 horsepower, new sport suspension and a Torsen® limited-slip differential. Plus, special features

gave it an

like a front air dam and rear spoiler. The 1994 Miata R Package. The only car that's racier is rated RX.

R rating.

IT JUST FEELS RIGHT.®

The Mazda MX-5 Miata has been an *Automobile Magazine* "All Star" for 5 consecutive years and is backed by a best-in-class, 36-month/50,000-mile, no-deductible, "bumper-to-bumper" limited basic warranty. See your Mazda Dealer for details. For a free brochure, call 1-800-639-1000. © 1994 Mazda Motor of America, Inc.

The R Package. Although officially announced at the 1994 Chicago Show, its sporty specification had been mentioned in the 1994 model year catalogue.

trimmed steering wheel, electric door mirrors, headrest speakers and (with manual transmission models) a Torsen differential. Package B had all the items in Package A plus cruise control, electric windows and an electric aerial. Package C came with everything in Package B plus a tan leather interior and matching soft-top. Separate options included air conditioning (at $830), ABS brakes ($900), the latest electronically controlled, four-speed automatic gearbox ($850), a body coloured hard-top ($1500), the Mazda Sensory Sound System with CD player ($700), cupholders, and floormats at just $65.

At the Chicago Auto Show, where the Mazda stand carried a couple of interesting alternative fuel MX-5s brought over from Japan, two new special Miatas were announced – the M Edition and the R Package. The 'limited production' M Edition (restricted to around 3000 units) was a luxury Miata finished in Montego Blue Mica ("a colour best described as twenty fathoms deep" according to Mazda's advertising material), with a tan leather interior and tan hood. Features included a polished version of

the regular seven-spoke alloys, a wooden gearknob and handbrake handle, electric windows and mirrors, air conditioning, central locking, stainless treadplates and a special keyfob. Weighing in at 1073kg (2360lb), it cost $21,675 – $4250 more than the base model at that time.

The R Package option was available as an upgrade on the basic car, priced at $1500. Stiffer springs, roll bars, bushings, and harder shock absorbers (sourced from Bilstein) gave the Miata R notably sharper handling, but a somewhat choppier ride. For the record, a 19mm (0.75in.) diameter anti-roll bar was the norm on US-spec cars, but it was upped to 20mm (0.79in.) on the R Package; the rear bar remained at 12mm (0.47in.), although regular cars without a limited-slip differential went to 11mm (0.43in.) for 1994, following the 1993 Limited Edition's lead. With its alloy wheels, Torsen limited-slip differential, front and rear spoilers and a reshaped rear valance, the R was a pure sports car. Luxury items such as power-assisted steering, an automatic transmission and ABS were not available – in fact, a stripe (designed by Mark

The 1995.5 model year Miata M Edition, the second in the M Edition run. This particular version was finished in Merlot Mica, whereas the first series had been painted in Montego Blue Mica. The colour would change for each season.

Jordan and listed at $230) and air conditioning were the only options.

Car & Driver found the R quicker off the line, but, more importantly, it was much better in manoeuvrability and slalom tests. It also recorded 0.86g on the skidpan against 0.83 for the M Edition. The magazine summed up the R with the comment: "The suspension glows on the track."

US sales for 1994 were almost the same as they had been in 1993 – at 21,400 units, there was a shortfall of only 188 cars on the previous year.

In competition, 1994 was the first year that the Sports Car Club of America moved its annual run-offs to Mid-Ohio (they had been held at Road Atlanta since 1970). The Miata duly took the SCCA Showroom Stock C title for the third year in a row (Michael Galati in car number 9 taking the chequered flag), while Terry McCarthy (car number 23) claimed the E-Production crown. Incidentally, the new 1.8-litre cars were placed in the Showroom Stock D category.

For the 1995 model year, it was decided to combine Package A and B to create a new option known as the Popular Equipment Package; Package C became known as the Leather Package, although the R Package (still for manual Miatas only) remained unchanged. The optional ABS braking system was now lighter than before, and Montego Blue Mica could be specified on all cars in the range unless they were fitted with the R Package.

Midway through 1995, Mazda introduced another special Miata M Edition. Finished in a striking Merlot Mica (a purple metallic shade), it was priced at $23,530. For that, the buyer got special seats with tan leather trim, 6J x 15 BBS alloys fitted with 195/55 tyres, ABS brakes, a limited-slip differential, Nardi black leather gearknob, polished treadplates, M Edition floormats, a CD player, air conditioning, and unique badging. A nice touch was the M Edition keyfob and lapel pin.

While sales in Canada were down to three figures, American sales for 1995 remained fairly constant, with just over 20,000 units being recorded for the year (of which, around 3500 of these were M Edition models).

The M-Speedster

The Miata M-Speedster made its debut at the 1995 Chicago Auto Show. It was designed by Wu-Huang Chin of MRA, and featured a supercharged 1.8-litre engine. To keep the 200 horses in check, 215/50 ZR15 tyres were employed, mounted on five-spoke alloy wheels. The suspension and braking system was also uprated, with 250mm (9.8in) ventilated discs at the front and 225mm (8.8in) solid discs at the rear.

Complete Car was quite confident that this vehicle gave an insight into the future, despite Tom Matano saying: "We have no intention of building it." Perhaps the magazine thought it was being used as a tool to gauge reaction, as at the end of the article, it said: "If US buyers give the thumbs up, it will form the blueprint for a revamp in Europe." Sadly, although there was almost universal praise for the machine, it turned out to be nothing more than a concept car.

The Miata M-Speedster made its debut at the 1995 Chicago Auto Show.

The aggresive lines of the M-Speedster, built on the so-called 'Mi-ari' – a one-off car produced by the Irvine team to honour Ferrari at Monterey in 1994. Twin round lamps were hidden under each headlight cover, and a pair of matching helmets nestled under the fairings behind the seats. Many thought that the M-Speedster would form the basis for the second generation MX-5.

Stunning interior of the M-Speedster.

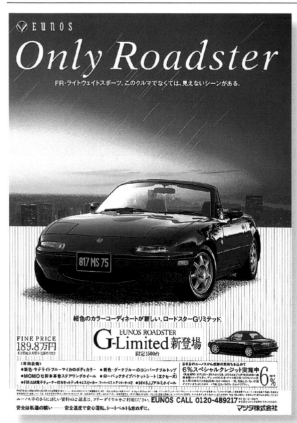

Japan's limited editions

Having seen how successful short run cars with various unique features could be in promoting sales for very little outlay, Mazda announced the 500-off RS Limited in July 1994. With sales starting in September, the 2,215,000 yen RS Limited was based on the S Special and finished in Montego Blue Mica. Interesting features included a lightened flywheel, a 4.3:1 final-drive ratio, Bridgestone Potenza RE010 tyres mounted on BBS 6J x 15 alloys, Recaro bucket seats, RS decals on the front wings, and a Nardi leather-trimmed, three-spoke steering wheel. However, despite Mazda's best efforts, sales fell again in Japan, 1994's total failing to break the 11,000 mark.

Undeterred, sales of the M Package-based G Limited began in January 1995. Priced at just under 1,900,000 yen in manual guise (an automatic was available on this model), only 1500 were built, all finished in Satellite Blue Mica with a dark blue hood. Low-back bucket seats, like those used in the J Limited II, were fitted, along with a new style Momo leather-covered steering wheel, seven-spoke alloy wheels, and an uprated sound system.

In the following month, the R Limited was introduced at 2,175,000 yen. Based on the S Special, the R Limited came in Satellite Blue Mica or Chaste White (of the 1000 built, the blue shade accounted for 894 sales) with a red leather interior. Like

This is the G Limited: a run of 1500 vehicles based on the M M Package. The special seats were trimmed in Alcantara.

Interior of the RS Limited, complete with its chunky yet lightweight Recaro seats.

The home market's RS Limited of 1994 vintage, restricted to just 500 examples.

The S Special-based R Limited. Almost 900 were produced in this dark blue shade, with the rest finished in white, to bring the total to 1000 units.

the RS Limited, it featured a lightened flywheel, 4.3:1 final-drive, BBS alloys and Potenza tyres, but this time had a wooden three-spoke Nardi steering wheel and gearknob, as well as wood trim on the handbrake lever.

By this time, Brilliant Black had joined the basic colour line-up, so buyers no longer had to order a limited edition or the V Special for the privilege of black coachwork; it became available from January '95. In addition, the S Special could be bought in Chaste White, thus giving three colour choices on that model instead of the previous two.

Britain in 1995

On 14 March, the California Limited Edition was launched at the Design Centre in London to celebrate the MX-5's fifth anniversary, although sales didn't start until 27 May. Based on the 1.8i model, all cars had Sunburst Yellow paintwork, power steering, 7J x 15 five-spoke alloy wheels, and a Clarion CRX601R radio/cassette unit. Only 300 of the £15,795 cars were made, all carrying a numbered plaque on the fascia and a 'California' badge mounted on the rear panel.

Ironically, with people complaining of a lack of power on the old 1.6-litre car, just as many campaigned for the return of the 1.6i, not least the marketing people at Mazda UK. Higher insurance rates and the escalation of list prices weren't exactly hurting sales (one would expect them to fall after an initial boom, and 1994's figures were actually an improvement on those from the previous two years), but the competition was starting to get its act together, particularly the Rover Group with its new MGF. A cheaper car in the line-up would certainly help the MX-5 maintain its market share.

On 12 April 1995, the 1.6i was re-introduced as the entry level model to complement the £14,495 1.8i and £17,395 1.8iS. The detuned 1598cc B6 engine produced only 88bhp but, priced at just £12,995, few complained. Naturally, the specification was pretty basic: 5.5J x 14 steel wheels, no power steering, manual windows, no radio/cassette, plus the suspension modifications and body-bracing found on the 1.8-litre models was omitted.

Oddly, the brake discs were reduced in diameter by 20mm (0.78in) all-round compared to the 1.8-litre cars

A rare publicity shot of the R Limited, dating from February 1995.

The California Limited Edition. Note the windscreen surround in body colour – the second version of the home market's J Limited had appeared with a black frame.

(the 1.6i's discs were, in effect, brought back down to the original dimensions), and it was initially only available in three colours: Classic Red, Brilliant Black, and Chaste White. However, an immobiliser was included as standard.

Shortly afterwards, *Complete Car* stated: "Mazda has cut the price of its cheapest MX-5 by nearly £1500 in a bid to beat competition from the new MGF. The MX-5, the biggest-selling open sports car in the world, is now available from £12,995 for the 1.6i – cheaper than the original MX-5 launched five years ago in Britain.

"Commenting on the launch of the Rover MGF, Mazda Cars UK boss David Heslop said he believed its arrival would expand the market for all sports cars. 'We're biased, but we think the MX-5 is a prettier car,' he added. 'And our research shows that real enthusiasts like the traditional formula of front engine and rear-wheel drive.'"

The sparring continued in a quality newspaper, with Rover bosses knocking the MX-5 by saying it had no pedigree, and therefore the MG was better. As a historian, I find it hard to believe that anyone could say Mazda is lacking in pedigree. The marque has achieved some excellent results in the American and European motorsport arenas (the RX-7 has notched up more IMSA wins than any other car in the history of the series), and the author witnessed the Hiroshima company's victory at the Le Mans 24-hour race in

The Mazdaspeed catalogue from mid-1995. A combination of the Mazdaspeed front spoiler and side skirts gave a drop in drag of around 7 per cent. Note the rather hefty Mazdaspeed anti-draft device behind the seats, fitted in conjunction with a rollbar.

Der Mazda MX-5

Although much of the photography had been seen before (and quite a lot of it was shared within Europe), at least each country had a unique mix and highlighted different features. On this page we can see the UK (top left), German (top right) and Dutch brochures from 1995. The German edition (printed in May) carried details on the 1.6-litre model, but the British and Dutch catalogues – although printed around the same time – left it out for the time being as it was not available until the end of the year. Occasionally, similar-looking brochures would appear in the Far East; Singapore listed the 1.8 with a five-speed manual or four-speed automatic transmission while, for a time, Hong Kong received the automatic only.

Britain's luxurious Gleneagles model (named after the world-famous golf course) was launched at the 1995 Earls Court Motor Show. One example was donated by Mazda UK in a bid to raise funds to help send Scottish athletes to the 1996 Olympics.

1991. So many companies have established themselves with good results at the famous Sarthe track, and some are still selling cars on the back of this reputation to this day. At the time, I was not an MX-5 fan, but I couldn't help asking myself if the MG marque had ever won outright at Le Mans!

The argument could go on forever, but there was no doubt that Mazda had a strong competitor in the MGF, which was due to be launched in August to coincide with the issue of the new registration letter.

In fact, despite all the column inches about the smaller-engined car, the 1.6i wasn't available until November (by which time it cost £500 more). Official figures on the 1.6i quoted 0-62mph (100kph) in 10.6 seconds and a top speed of 109mph (174kph). In the meantime, in mid-1995, the 1.8iS received a restyled steering wheel (complete with airbag); in addition, another limited edition car was on its way.

At the 1995 Earls Court Motor Show, Mazda UK launched the 1.8-litre Gleneagles. Based on the 1.8i, the Gleneagles was finished in Montego Blue and, although the hood itself was black, it came with a champagne-coloured hood cover to match the interior. Priced at £16,465, it had power-assisted steering, leather seats, attractive 15-inch five-spoke alloys, a Momo leather-trimmed steering wheel (with the Gleneagles emblem on the boss), a wood effect console, a CD player, Gleneagles tartan trim on the gearlever gaiter, and, of course, special 'Gleneagles' badging.

Mazda UK Ltd later donated a Gleneagles model to the British Olympic Appeal to help send Scottish athletes to the 1996 Atlanta Olympics. It was hoped that £250,000 could be raised through the sale of lottery tickets – was this the most expensive MX-5 ever?

The November 1995 issue of *Complete Car* pitted the MX-5 1.8iS against the new front-wheel drive Alfa

Another shot of the MX-5 Gleneagles.

Romeo Spider (eventually launched in the UK in spring 1996, at £22,000), the £15,995 1.8-litre fuel-injected MGF, and Fiat's recently announced Barchetta, priced at £13,995. Tony Dron, a classic car enthusiast and ex-BTCC Champion, noted that the MX-5 "looks a little dated now, but [it is] still a yardstick by which to judge these new sports cars."

The article went on to say that "driven fast, the Mazda does not roll excessively: it turns into corners well, understeering mildly at normal speeds. Push it a little harder and it's quite easy to provoke a mild and easily controlled tail slide which requires simple throttle control. Overdo it and you might spin but it is relatively easy to drive the Mazda in this entertaining fashion."

The Mazda was the lightest of the bunch (by over 40kg, or 88lb), but it was the slowest, and only the Alfa was worse on overall fuel consumption. Despite a number of compliments for the Hiroshima-built machine, in the end it was placed third, the MG taking the spoils with the Fiat runner-up.

In its September 1995 issue, *Car & Driver* compared the MX-5 (in Italian specification) with the Alfa Romeo Spider and Fiat Barchetta on home ground. The general concensus was that the Mazda was starting to show its age against the Italian newcomers, "but it's still a performer, and a beauty in profile." Perhaps the competition was starting to catch up?

One thing the *Complete Car* article highlighted was how little the MX-5 weighed. The 1.6i was naturally the lightest car in the range, tipping the scales at just 965kg (2123lb). The 1.8i was 25kg (55lb) heavier, while the 1.8iS weighed just over a ton, at 1018kg (2240lb). All were extremely light by the day's standards.

By the end of the year, the changes for 1996 were already filtering through. Armrests came back in preference to the unpopular door pockets, instruments lost their chrome ring surrounds, and the 1.8iS radio/cassette unit was changed. Laguna Blue was deleted from the colour charts, leaving Classic Red, British Racing Green, Silver Stone Metallic, Brilliant Black and Chaste White, although the BRG and silver shades were still not available on the 1.6i model.

Amazingly, MX-5 mania seemed to gather pace again. In 1995, Mazda UK sold 17,775 vehicles (only a few short of the total for 1994), but MX-5 sales almost doubled – no less than 2495 found homes during the year. These were the best results in the UK to date, although most other markets recorded a fall in sales; the rest of Europe could only muster 5221 sales in 1995.

More changes in Japan

August 1995 saw the introduction of the 133bhp Series II 1.8-litre engine. Although the BP-ZE (RS) designation was retained, the Series II version featured a 16-bit

ECU (Electronic Control Unit) and a lightweight flywheel to enable the engine to rev more freely. The 4.3:1 final-drive ratio was brought back on five-speed cars, although automatic models stayed at 4.1:1, and the Torsen LSD was modified.

An airbag was now standard on all Roadsters, the original, low mounted interior lights were replaced by a single unit by the relocated rearview mirror, the chrome dial surrounds were deleted, the sunvisors became a simple one-piece affair, door pockets were reduced in size (and not fitted at all on the basic car, or those with the polished speaker surround plates), trim material and door furniture was revised (bringing back armrests at the same time), and the colour of the 'Roadster' script found on the rear panel was changed from red to green.

Production of the Series II cars started on chassis NA8C-400007 and, as usual in Japan, the line-up was an extensive one. The standard model remained in manual guise only, becoming even more basic (even the hood cover was optional), but it was available in the full range of colours: Classic Red, Chaste White, Silver Stone Metallic, Brilliant Black and Neo Green.

The Special Package model remained the most popular, with prices starting at 1,930,000 yen for the manual version or 1,980,000 yen for the automatic. The Special Package came with alloy wheels, power steering, Torsen differential (manual cars), a new stereo radio/cassette unit, electrically adjustable door mirrors, electric windows, and a new leather-trimmed, three-spoke steering wheel, complete with airbag, of course.

In between the base model and the Special Package, there was now the 1,790,000 yen M Package. At 100,000 yen more than the basic Roadster, it had steel wheels and the basic three-spoke steering wheel, but featured power-assisted steering, electric windows and a decent stereo system.

The V Special grade was retained (starting at 2,300,000 yen), as was the V Special Type II with its unique features (again, it was 100,000 yen more). Colour options were restricted to just Brilliant Black, Neo Green and Chaste White on these models, and they came with a new three-spoke, wood-rimmed steering wheel from Nardi.

August 1995 saw the introduction of the Series II cars, powered by an uprated version of the 1.8-litre engine that had been adopted across the range two years earlier. This is the Japanese Special Package model.

A delightful publicity shot from autumn 1995 featuring the Special Package model.

The 1800 Series II range in Japan, and its leading features.

The V Special Type II from the same era.

The S Special Type II of late 1995 vintage.

The wine red VR Limited Combination A. Just 700 of these S Special Type I-based cars were produced, with sales starting in January 1996.

Finished in dark green, this is the VR Limited Combination B. Launched alongside the Combination A model, 800 examples were built.

An advert for the home market VR Limited Combination A and Combination B models. The wheels were later adopted as standard on the UK specification 1998 model year 1.8iS.

Excellent Green Mica. This model had a dark green soft-top, black leather interior, and the same alloy gearknob, shift plate and handbrake. Although based on the Type I, both cars had five-spoke 6J x 15 alloys instead of the familiar seven-spoke items.

Despite the many changes in the range – and the special editions – sales continued to decline rapidly in Japan. In fact, only 7178 Mazda roadsters were sold on the home market during 1995. This meant that, for the first time, European sales figures had exceeded those of Japan.

America in 1996

The 1996 model year line-up was announced in October 1995. Engine power increased to 133bhp, but the main changes centred on meeting new regulations – namely, the 1997 Federal side impact requirements and OBD-II emissions. Other, more minor, changes included relocation of the interior lights, a black hazard light switch to replace the old red one and the addition of a small light in the boot.

The three option packages from 1995 were available again (the Popular Equipment Package, the Leather Package and the R Package), but there was now also a Power Steering Package that added just power-assisted steering and wheel trim rings to the basic car; it was priced at a very reasonable $300, while the base model came in at $18,750.

To recap, the $2090 Popular Equipment Package included alloy wheels, power-assisted steering, a leather-wrapped steering wheel, cruise control, power windows and mirrors, headrest speakers, an electric aerial, and a limited-slip differential on cars with a manual transmission (those with an automatic gearbox had to do without the lsd, but the PEP option came $390 cheaper).

The $2985 Leather Package included a tan interior with leather seat facings and a matching tan hood, while the $1500 R Package featured alloy wheels, a Torsen lsd, uprated suspension components (including Bilstein dampers), front and rear skirts, and a rear spoiler.

As for individual options, air conditioning was listed at $900, as were ABS brakes, the hard-top was $1500, and an automatic gearbox cost $850. The $875 MSSS was now augmented by the Mazda Premium Sound System which, at $675, boasted a CD player and uprated speakers. Floormats rounded off the options list, priced at $80.

Only four colours were listed as standard: Classic Red, Brilliant Black, White and Montego Blue Mica – the latter taking the place of Laguna Blue on the colour palette during the 1995 season. These were available across the range, with the exception of the blue shade, which couldn't be specified with the R Package.

Road & Track observed: "Now approaching its sixth birthday, the Mazda Miata hasn't lost a bit of the shine it possessed when it rolled into our hands and hearts in the

The manual only S Special was also continued at 1,995,000 yen, but there was now an S Special Type II at 190,000 yen more. The extra money gave Potenza RE010 tyres mounted on 6J x 15 BBS alloy wheels (the run-of-the-mill Type I had the usual 14-inch, seven-spoke alloys, which Kijima-san thought was the best combination). Incidentally, the S Special cars were available in either Montego Blue Mica, Brilliant Black, Chaste White or Classic Red.

At the end of the year, Mazda announced the VR Limited Combination A and Combination B models; sales of these interesting variations – both based on the S Special Type I – started in January 1996. The Combination A (priced at 2,080,000 yen and limited to 700 cars) was finished in wine red with a tan coloured soft-top and matching leather-trimmed interior; an aluminium alloy gearknob, shift plate and handbrake lever were used for the first time. The Combination B was the same price, but limited to 800 examples, and came in a shade known as

The M-Coupé

The M-Coupé was the third Miata-based concept car by MRA, making its debut at the New York International Auto Show in April 1996. It resembled the M2-1008 above the waistline, but was much closer to standard below it.

There were differences, of course: twin round headlights hid under each pop-up cover (which looked very attractive), and there was a feature line running from the sill to just behind the door. The lines of the fibreglass roof panel merged beautifully with the rest of the body – the design was a credit to Tom Matano and his team.

This elegant coupé was powered by the stock B6-ZE engine linked to a five-speed gearbox; 205/45 R16 Dunlop SP8000 tyres were employed, mounted on lightweight five-spoke alloy wheels. An interesting feature was the increased luggage space, created by moving the spare wheel to an underfloor position.

Again, Matano stressed that the M-Coupé was only ever meant to be a styling exercise, but the favourable reaction it received from the public fuelled rumours it might go into production. It never did.

The M-Coupé was first shown at the 1996 New York Show. The roof on this model was made from fibreglass but, had it gone into production, steel would have been used instead. Unlike the coupé developed by the M2 team, the rear lights on the MRA machine were standard Miata fare.

This picture, taken by the author at MRA during a trip to California, shows the M-Speedster and M-Coupe as they looked in 2004, seen here with the Mono-Posto Concept on the right.

The 1996.5 model year Miata M Edition (the third in the series), finished in Starlight Mica.

Another view of the 1996.5 model year Miata M Edition. The interior featured tan leather trim (the seats being embossed with the 'Miata' logo), along with a wooden gearknob and handbrake garnish, and a leather-wrapped steering wheel.

Announced at the same time as the B2 Limited, the R2 Limited was based on the S Special Type I. R2 stood for Racy & Red (the red referring to the car's interior); production was limited to just 500 units.

Red and racy interior of the R2 Limited.

Introduced in December 1996, the B2 Limited was based on the M Package model. Restricted to 1000 examples, the B2 designation stood for Blue & Bright.

late 1980s. Lightweight, front-engine/rear-drive roadsters with looks to charm and personality to spare, new Miatas are still affordable and used ones are bargains (and well looked after by their loving owners). If you can't have fun in this car, maybe you belong somewhere in a Dickens novel."

Midway through 1996, the $24,760 Miata M Edition appeared in Starlight Mica, an attractive dark blue metallic shade found on the Millennia saloon. Trimmed in tan leather with a matching tan coloured hood and hood cover, the high spec package included such niceties as 15-inch five-spoke Enkei alloys (fitted with 195/50 tyres), a limited-slip differential, ABS brakes, air conditioning, a top stereo unit with CD player, headrest speakers and an electric aerial, cruise control, a Nardi wooden gearknob and handbrake handle, a leather-trimmed steering wheel, power windows and mirrors, stainless treadplates, an 'M Edition' logo on the tachometer, a remote keyless entry system, and an alarm. The only options were automatic transmission and a hard-top, as virtually everything else seemed to be fitted anyway.

The USA took another 18,408 Miatas during 1996 (the M Edition accounted for 2968 of these). This meant the running total for American sales now stood at a massive 196,770 units, a figure that represented some 48 per cent of production at that time.

The Land of the Rising Sun in 1996

Mazda built a total of 1,197,872 vehicles in 1987, of which over two-thirds were passenger cars. Production figures rose to a peak of 1,422,624 in 1990 before falling back to just over one million in 1993.

After that, production continued to fall, with only 773,567 vehicles being built in 1996 (around 600,000 were passenger cars, with well over half of them being exported). The MX-5 accounted for less than 1 per cent of this figure but, by the end of the year, cumulative production of the MX-5 had reached more than 400,000 units (the 400,000th vehicle was built on 2 November 1996). The RX-7 had already surpassed 1,000,000 units by this time, although it had been on sale since 1978, of course.

In 1996, the Eunos sales outlets were integrated into the Mazda Anfini, Mazda or Ford dealerships, the Eunos Roadster being sold through the Mazda Anfini sales channel, lining up alongside the RX-7, MS8, MPV and Eunos Presso. The Anfini network boasted 87 dealers with a total of 633 outlets across Japan, but annual sales

figures were still dismal, with fewer than 4500 cars finding homes during the year.

At the end of 1996, in December, all models adopted a new Momo four-spoke steering wheel (with airbag), and two more limited edition Eunos Roadsters came along: the B2 Limited at 1,898,000 yen (or 1,993,000 with automatic transmission) and the manual only R2 Limited at 2,098,000 yen.

Based on the M Package, B2 apparently stood for Blue & Bright, although the Twilight Blue Mica shade chosen for the vehicle was hardly the brightest in the Mazda range, and the black interior was rather austere to say the least. Anyway, limited to 1000 examples, the main features included a dark blue soft-top, highly-polished 14-inch seven-spoke alloys, chrome door mirrors, moquette-trimmed bucket seats, chrome dial surrounds, and a combined CD/cassette/radio unit. Air conditioning was available as an option.

The 500-off R2 Limited (which was based on the S Special Type I) came in Chaste White, despite the R2 appellation standing for Racy & Red! This was actually a reference to the red and black interior, which included red leather seats. Bridgestone Potenza tyres came on 6J x 15 five-spoke alloys, while the aluminium alloy gearknob, shift plate and handbrake lever were revived, along with the chrome dial surrounds found on the B2 version.

The British market in 1996

A Mazda UK press release in 1996 described the salient features of the MX-5 in the following terms: "The race-bred induction system, distributor-less ignition and lightweight flywheel ensure a quick, lively throttle response ... The drivetrain is locked in rigid alignment by means of an ingenious aluminium powerplant frame. Suspension is all-independent, using double-wishbones and anti-roll bars, while a brace bar and performance

A British spec 1.8i model dating from the early part of 1996. This car is painted in Classic Red; other colours included Brilliant Black, Chaste White, Silver Stone Metallic, and British Racing Green, although the latter two were not available on the 1.6i. Note the standard steel wheels.

The 1.8iS model from the same period, with alloy wheels as standard.

The Merlot (right) was launched in the UK in mid-1996 alongside the smaller-engined Monaco. It came with a luxurious grey leather trim, wood finish to the dashboard, and a leather-wrapped steering wheel; a CD player also came as standard. Although both models had five-spoke alloy wheels, they were actually slightly different in design.

rods increase body rigidity on 1.8i models for enhanced chassis control.

"The rack-and-pinion steering has just 3.3 turns lock-to-lock and with power assistance on the 1.8iS this is reduced to 2.8. Braking is by discs all-round, ventilated at the front, solid at the back, and reinforced by ABS on the 1.8iS.

"For security, all models are fitted with an engine immobiliser, security-coded window etching, lockable glovebox and central storage box, and remote fuel flap releases.

"The plastic nose section is designed to resist stone chips and incorporates pop-up halogen headlamps. Everything is set up for a sporty experience: the tightly grouped pedals and dials, leather steering wheel on the 1.8iS, the driver's left foot rest.

"But safety is built in, too, from the side impact door beams and energy absorbing bumpers to the flame retardant trim and upholstery. A driver's side airbag and anti-lock braking are standard on the 1.8iS, which offers additional luxury with its detachable RDS radio/cassette, alloy wheels, electric windows and door mirrors, and remote boot opening."

On 12 June 1996, Mazda UK announced two new limited edition models – the MX-5 1.6 Monaco and the MX-5 1.8 Merlot. From the press release, it was obvious that these latest additions were aimed squarely at a certain Rover Group product: "The Mazda MX-5 Monaco costs £13,750 – which is £2645 below the price of the cheapest MGF – while the high specification MX-5 Merlot costs nearly £2500 less than the MGF VVC, at £16,350.

"Finished in British Racing Green and fitted with a tan hood, the Monaco is mechanically identical to the MX-5 1.6i. Special features of this limited edition roadster include alloy wheels and a radio/cassette player. The MX-5 Monaco has a top speed of 109mph [174kph] and accelerates from 0-62mph [100kph] in 10.6 seconds. It achieves 42.2mpg at a steady 56mph [90kph].

"The luxurious Merlot – which has a special deep lustrous red body colour called Vin Rouge – has [light grey] leather upholstery, quality wood trim, a CD sound system, alloy wheels and power-assisted steering, [along with a Momo leather-trimmed steering wheel]. The 1.8-litre, 16v engine develops 131bhp to give acceleration from 0-62mph [100kph] in 8.6 seconds plus a top speed of 123mph [197kph]. It returns more than 40mpg in the steady 56mph [90kph] test."

Although Australian sales picked up very slightly

Cover shot from the 1997 model year Miata catalogue. This was the last one produced for the first generation car as there wasn't a 1998 model year vehicle for the States.

The Australian market's 1.8 Limited Edition, restricted to just 75 units. Launched in January 1996, it was finished in Neo Green with a tan leather interior and tan hood cover; the wheels were the familiar seven-spoke production items. Sadly, despite the introduction of a number of special versions over the years, sales in Australia remained low.

(241 units for the year, taking the running total for that country to 4609), Europe was the only market to show a notable improvement. In Britain, MX-5 sales continued to strengthen. During 1996, Mazda UK had a bumper year, selling no fewer than 3855 examples of the popular convertible. The European mainland recorded 5730 sales, bringing the total for the whole of Europe to a healthy 9585 units (more than twice the figure for the home market during the same period).

The American scene

In 1997, the MX-5 Miata was included in the American *Automobile* magazine's 'All Stars' listing for the seventh consecutive year, although the $19,675 price tag (including delivery charges) was a far cry from that advertised at the start of the decade. 1997's colour schemes remained the same as for the 1996 model year, but the options were revised once again.

The Power Steering Package included power-assisted steering and wheel trim rings, while the new Touring Package listed power steering, a leather-wrapped steering wheel, electric windows, electrically adjustable door mirrors, alloy wheels and door pockets. The latest Popular Equipment Package had everything in the Touring Package, plus a Torsen limited-slip differential (for manual cars), the rear subframe performance rods, speakers in the headrests, cruise control and an electric aerial. The Leather Package built on the Popular Equipment Package with a tan leather interior and tan vinyl top. The R Package (for manual cars only) incorporated uprated suspension

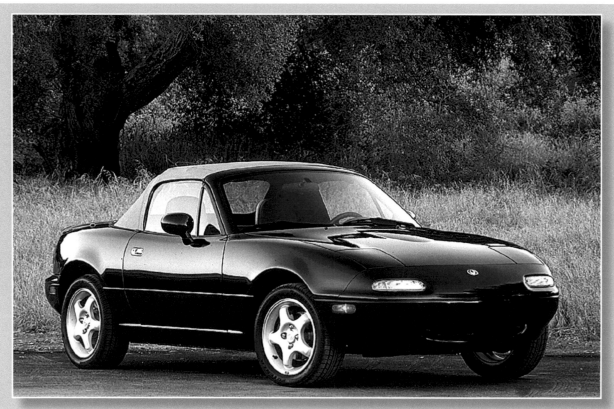

Two views of the well-equipped Miata STO Edition which was announced in July 1997. STO stood for Special Touring Option, by the way.

IN OUR
NEWEST GREEN,
YOU'LL DETECT
SHADES OF
THE PAST.

MAZDA MIATA
1997 M EDITION.

The M Edition for 1997, the fourth in the series, was finished in Marina Green Mica. The first had been painted in Montego Blue Mica, while those that followed came in Merlot Mica and Starlight Mica, respectively.

Part of the Swiss MX-5 catalogue dating from early 1997. Note the different five-spoke alloy wheels available on the so-called HE version.

The 1.8-litre MX-5 Dakar, 400 of which were built for the British market. The advertising stated: "This car will become a timeless classic ..."

with Bilstein shock absorbers, rear subframe performance rods, a Torsen lsd, front and rear spoilers, a rear skirt, and alloy wheels with locking wheelnuts.

Separate options included a detachable hard-top, air conditioning, four-sensor, three-channel ABS brakes, the 160W Mazda Premium Sound System, and a four-speed automatic transmission with 'Hold' facility. Accessories, such as polished alloys, stainless treadplates, racing stripes, a boot-mounted luggage rack, rear spoiler, aero parts kit, tonneau cover, front 'bra,' foglights and a CD changer, were also offered by dealerships.

Priced at $24,485 and limited to 3000 units, the M Edition for the 1997 model year was finished in a shade known as Marina Green Mica on this occasion, an attractive dark green colour set off by the contrasting tan leather trim and hood. Other features included highly polished, 15-inch, six-spoke alloy wheels, stainless treadplates, custom floormats, Nardi wooden gearknob and handbrake trim, a CD player attached to the MPSS audio system, air conditioning, and special badging.

A press release dated 1 July described the latest American special edition – the $22,520 STO Edition. It read: "Arriving just in time to make the most of warm summer nights throughout the country, Mazda has announced the addition of a new limited production version of the company's classic roadster – the 1997.5 MX-5 Miata STO Edition. The STO stands for Special Touring Option, a combination of popular options that embodies the true lightweight, affordable sports car spirit of the Miata ... Only 1500 of the Miata STO Edition [models] will be produced.

"Highlighting the 1997.5 STO Edition is Twilight Blue Mica paint, topped off by a tan leather interior and tan vinyl top. In addition to the unique paint scheme, the STO Edition features special Enkei 15-inch wheels and low-profile 50-series tyres; rear lip spoiler; STO Edition

The English Mazda range for the 1997 season, including the 323, the MX-5, 626, and MX-6.

logos on the floormats; Nardi leather shift knob (manual transmission only); stainless steel scuff plates; an STO Edition sequentially numbered dash plaque, and certificate of authenticity.

"The car is also equipped with a full complement of luxury features, including headrest speakers, leather-wrapped steering wheel, power mirrors, power windows and a CD player. The only options are air conditioning and a four-speed automatic transmission."

Just over 17,000 Miatas were sold in the States during 1997 (although only 11,950 were officially exported to America that year, along with a further 618 for Canada), while in SCCA racing, the Miata resumed its winning ways after a couple of lean years – Pratt Cole took the E-Production title and Michael Galati claimed Showroom Stock B honours.

The situation in the UK

By this time, the Mazda had a whole string of competitors to contend with. The BMW Z3 was another newcomer (albeit a more expensive one), but, comparing it to the MX-5, Gavin Conway of *Autocar* said: "The Z3 has more cabin space, better performance, more mature yet still enjoyable handling, and a much bigger dose of badge pride."

In January 1997, the 400-off Dakar Limited Edition was announced. Priced at £17,210 on the road, it was finished in Twilight Blue Metallic, with the interior in mid-grey leather with dark blue piping. Other features included unique 15-inch, 16-spoke alloy wheels, burr walnut trim, a chrome rear brace bar, chrome treadplates, a Momo leather-trimmed steering wheel, Dakar floormats in grey with dark blue edging, a radio/cassette unit, and power-assisted steering. Each vehicle had a numbered plaque and 'Dakar' badging.

By spring 1997, a high level brake light had found its way onto the bootlid; the interior light was now incorporated into a new rearview mirror, and the 1.8i now had the same boot release arrangement as that found on the 1.8iS.

One of the last 1.8iS models to wear the now-familiar seven-spoke alloys. In October (for the 1998 model year in effect), the new five-spoke alloy wheels were adopted. The eagle-eyed will notice the fatter base on the door mirrors for cars with electrically-adjustable mirrors.

The MX-5 Classic, launched in the UK in October 1997.

Mazda UK's third special edition model of 1997 – the 1.8-litre Harvard.

The 1.6-litre Monza reached the UK market in May 1997. Finished in British Racing Green, this particular model was limited to 800 examples.

On 16 May 1997, Mazda UK announced the special edition MX-5 Monza. Named after the famous Italian racing circuit, the Monza was finished in British Racing Green and priced at £14,595. Limited to just 800 examples, it featured 14-inch, five-spoke alloy wheels with locking wheelnuts, an uprated sound system, and exclusive Monza badging, in addition to the standard equipment of the 1.6i upon which it was based.

A fortnight later, on 29 May, this was followed by the MX-5 Harvard. Based on the MX-5 1.8i in Silver Stone Metallic, it was equipped with power steering, 15-inch, five-spoke alloy wheels, burgundy leather upholstery with grey piping, a CD player, immobiliser, chrome brace bar, wood trim, a Momo leather-wrapped steering wheel, high level stop lamp, locking wheelnuts, polished treadplates, and special floormats with the Harvard logo.

The Harvard was priced at £17,495. To put this into perspective, the July price list quoted £14,410 for the 1.6i, the 1.8i was exactly £1000 more, while the 1.8iS was £18,510. Mica and metallic paint finishes cost £250 extra, leather trim added £923 to the invoice, and air conditioning (available on the 1.8-litre cars only) was a hefty £1395.

In October 1997, the final changes were made to take the car into 1998 until the new model's introduction. Both the 1.6i and 1.8i received power steering as standard, and the 1.8iS wheels were changed to 6J x 15 five-spoke alloys – almost the same design as those found on the Harvard but with dished centres.

At the same time, the 1.8i-based MX-5 Classic was launched. Finished in Brilliant Black, it featured black leather seat facings with red stitching, 15-inch,

five-spoke alloy wheels with locking wheelnuts, wood trim, a stainless steel rear brace bar, polished treadplates, a Momo leather-trimmed steering wheel, floormats in black with red edging, 'Classic' badging, and an RDS radio/cassette unit. It was priced at £17,495 on the road.

Sales throughout the British Isles continued to rise at a staggering rate. Accounting for almost exactly half of Europe's sales during 1997, Mazda UK sold 4956 MX-5s, bringing the running total to an impressive 18,715 units.

The final version of the first generation MX-5 was announced in January 1998 – the limited edition Berkeley, finished in Sparkle Green Metallic. Only 400 were produced, and the leading features were a black leather interior with contrasting light grey on the seat facings and door panels, 15-inch, five-spoke alloy wheels with locking wheelnuts, a chrome boot rack, a stainless steel rear brace bar, stainless treadplates, dark burr wood trim, a Momo leather-wrapped steering wheel, black leather gearlever and handbrake gaiter, a CD player, and black floormats edged in grey. A numbered plaque was mounted on the centre console, and 'Berkeley' badges were fitted just below the side repeater indicators on the front wings. The Berkeley was priced at a very reasonable £17,600.

Mazda MX-5 Berkeley

The 400-off Berkeley was announced in January 1998, and was the UK's final version of the first generation MX-5. Finished in Sparkle Green Metallic and with a black and grey leather interior, it was priced at £17,600, and was basically very similar to Japan's SR Limited model.

The home market

The range for the 1997 model year was unchanged from that which resulted from the reshuffle in the latter half of 1995; standard colour schemes were also unaltered. Prices had risen slightly over the last couple of years, but not by a great deal compared with those of the export markets. For instance, the basic model was 1,770,000 yen in Chiba (the author's home town in Japan, near to Tokyo) in December 1996, while, at the other end of the scale, the V Special Type II started at 2,470,000 yen.

In August 1997, the SR Limited was announced to celebrate the eighth anniversary of the Eunos Roadster in Japan. Based on the M Package, the manual version (with Torsen limited-slip differential) weighed exactly 1000kg (2200lb) and was priced at 1,898,000 yen; the automatic weighed 30kg (66lb) more and cost 1,978,000 yen.

Two colour options were available: Sparkle Green Metallic (the same colour as that seen on the British Berkeley) and Chaste White (of the 700 examples produced, white was the most popular shade, accounting for 384 sales). The standard Momo steering wheel with airbag was employed (shortly after the launch of the SR Limited, dual airbags became an option), but it had highly polished, seven-spoke alloys, black leather seats with light grey nubuck type inserts, chrome door mirrors, chrome dial surrounds, a CD/tuner, and a Nardi leather gearknob to distinguish it from the rest of the line-up.

By this time, more than enough cars had been sold on the home market to ascertain the various trends. The Special Package was the most popular model, accounting for roughly 40 per cent of sales. Japanese buyers usually prefer automatics, although only around 15 per cent of the Eunos Roadsters sold featured an automatic transmission. The most popular colour, however, would not surprise anyone who has lived in Japan – it was white. Next in line was green, followed by black.

Japanese sales figures released for December 1997 confirmed the growing popularity of utility vehicles and MPVs in preference to sports cars and coupés. The best-seller in the sporting sector was the Toyota Corolla Levin

Japan's SR Limited – the last special edition model for the home market. This example is shown in Sparkle Green Metallic but Chaste White was also available. In all, only 700 cars were built, with the white shade being the most popular colour.

The SR Limited in Chaste White.

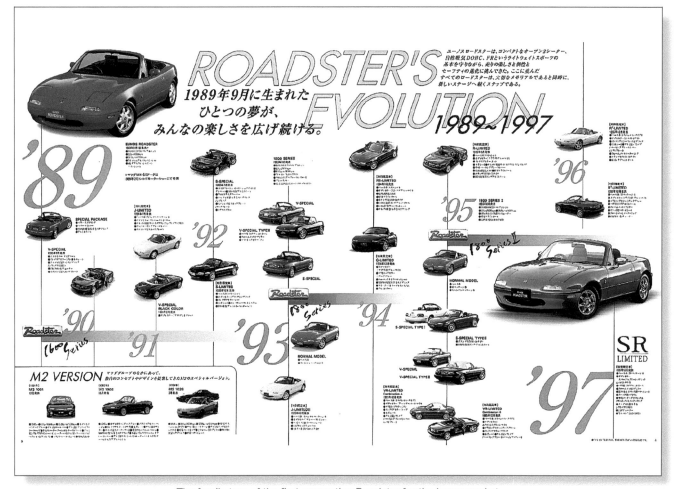

The family tree of the first generation Roadster for the home market.

with 722 units for the month; the Celica managed 464 sales, while the Supra clocked up just 145 – the MR2 recorded a disappointing 91 sales. Mazda was also struggling, with sales of 206 Eunos Roadsters and 202 RX-7s. The Nissan 300ZX and the rest of the Fairlady Z range found just 40 customers, although this was still quite a lot compared to sales of Honda's NSX supercar, which amounted to only 13 units.

By comparison, Honda sold 4230 of its CR-V and no less than 11,123 of its StepWgn people mover. In the smaller MPV class, Suzuki sold over 16,000 Wagon R models. Even executive cars were outselling sporting machines at a rate of almost ten to one! As the world's most dedicated followers of fashion, the Japanese were clearly telling the manufacturers that the sports car era was well and truly over unless they were offered something new: Eunos Roadster sales for the year added up to just 3537 units.

Fortunately, Mazda had a new model. The second generation MX-5 was eagerly awaited and, at the 1997 Tokyo Show, the car everyone wanted to see was finally unveiled.

Enthusiasts were pleased to see there were no compromises on the 'Jinba-ittai' philosophy developed by Hirai and his team, which called for a lightweight machine with equal weight distribution, a double-wishbone suspension, a low centre of gravity, a low yaw moment of inertia, the engine placed as far back as possible, a PPF brace, and an easy-to-use top. These features would ultimately be carried through from one MX-5 generation to the next.

However, it was the original MX-5 that had started a roadster renaissance. It also left a lasting impression, making it into the final cut of 100 cars put forward for the 'Car of the Century' title – one of only seven Japanese models (the Lexus LS400, Honda NSX, and the first generation of Toyota Corolla, Honda Civic, Datsun Z and Mazda RX-7 made up the total) left in with a chance. The Mini was ultimately declared the winner, a choice which the author finds very hard to understand ...

APPENDIX 1

Only a few months after the MX-5 was announced, *Road & Track* was predicting a boom for custom parts. In the July 1989 edition, the magazine said: "Mazda has set up the stock Miata for comfort more than handling. The ride is comfortably soft with more body roll than we would have expected. All of this is not to say that the Miata, with its light weight and short wheelbase, isn't quick and responsive; it's both. But it could be quicker and even more responsive. Already it is easy to see the aftermarket explosion this car is going to cause."

This observation was very astute. Today, as well as a thriving custom scene, there's no shortage of companies around the world which supply enthusiasts with accessories. This chapter looks briefly at what can only be described as the MX-5 'industry.'

Parts & accessories

In Japan, the choice of parts and accessories is huge. During 1994, Mazdaspeed, TRD (of Toyota fame) and Nismo (Nissan Motorsports International), joined forces to organise the Tokyo Auto Salon, an alternative motor show that caters purely for tuning and performance companies. In 1997, Mitsubishi Ralliart added its weight to the alliance, which duly adopted the 'Works Tuning' banner.

Apart from promoting the tuning business, Works Tuning also organises motorsport events in which owners can drive their cars at speed in controlled conditions. After all, if a person fits high quality performance parts, it

follows that he or she is going to want to try them out! The worthy objective behind the track days is to enhance the experience of responsible drivers and persuade the likes of Zero-Yon road racers (who illegally speed on public roads) to adopt a more suitable arena in which to enjoy their vehicles.

The author went to the 1997 Tokyo Auto Salon and was amazed at how big the event was. With around 900 cars on display, it attracted almost as many visitors as the Tokyo Show! The range of body kits, tuning parts and complete conversions was staggering; some of the modifications are quite tasteful, others totally over-the-top.

As well as Mazdaspeed, some of the better known concerns dealing with the Hiroshima marque included VeilSide, HKS, Racing Sports Active, KG Works, Hayashi, Manatee, Garage Vary, Yours Sports, Dave Crockett and RE Amemiya Cars, but the list was practically endless. Indeed, Hyper Rev managed to put together a book listing and describing the Eunos tuning scene in Japan which amounted to over 200 pages!

Trust of Chiba developed a turbo kit, and a company called Cockpit even offered an MX-5 fitted with a 400bhp rotary engine. Knight Sports, well known for its work on the RX-7, was also involved in supplying performance parts for the Roadster.

The owners' clubs also got involved. One club, known as Barchetta, designed and marketed its own

Advertising from the HKS concern. The car seen in the bottom left-hand corner is the T-003.

VeilSide of Tsukuba offers a wide range of conversions on various popular Japanese sports cars. This is the company's stunning Roadster Combat Model.

parts. A front fibreglass half-spoiler and bumper cover was available for 60,000 yen, while the attractive rear bumper was 100,000 yen. Smaller items were also listed, such as a gearshift gate box at just 6000 yen.

HKS offered a full T-003 conversion, and Pit Crew Racing's modifications made the Eunos look like an early TVR. Zoom designed a fairly convincing Lotus Elan lookalike, while others offered nose panels that were shaped to resemble different vehicles, ranging from the Ferrari Daytona through to the Nissan 300ZX. One concern even built a nose that reminded the author of a cross between the Daimler SP250 and Austin-Healey Sprite.

Of course, the full custom scene is much stronger in Japan where the cars are so much cheaper to buy. In Britain, the purchase price and high residual value on the second-hand car market puts most people off the idea of modifying their car too much, as it would affect the price when they came to sell it.

However, subtle modifications are commonplace. The industry supplying somewhat more restrained

aftermarket components has blossomed, and the variety already rivals that for some of the more established 'classics' for range. For instance, the catalogue issued by Moss International Ltd (ironically, a company better known for supplying parts for classic British marques such as MG and Triumph!) lists items like stainless steel exhaust systems and replacement catalytic converters, high performance air filters, sparkplugs and leads, silicone hoses and a gel cell battery. Naturally, these are joined by uprated suspension and braking components, including strut tower and chassis braces.

For the interior, there are leather seats, real or fake wood trim kits, various gearknobs and steering wheels, and leather gaiters for the gearlever and handbrake. Kits are also available for interior lighting, electric windows, central and remote keyless locking, and an electronic boot release. There are also floor mats, stainless steel trim pieces for the sill tops, face vents and speakers, and an aluminium pedal set. The catalogue also lists replacement soft-tops, a hard-top, wind deflector, boot spoiler, various

The brochure from KG Works of Yokohama. The M-Coupé-style, twin headlight conversion (priced at 128,000 yen) is very elegant. Japan is full of companies like this offering body kits, cosmetic parts and tuning components. To list them all would take a book in itself!

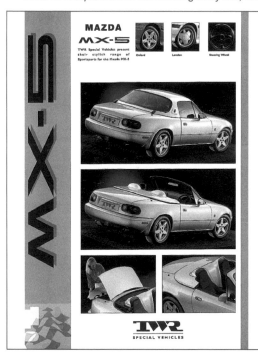

luggage racks and boot trim components, including a hydraulic lift kit. Auxilliary lighting, a protective front grille, roll-over bar, car cover, Minilite-style alloys, and a 7.5J x 16 wheel and tyre package make up the selection on offer.

Of course, the Moss catalogue is only one of many: Mazda lists the Finish Line range of accessories, which includes items such as a detachable hard-top, alloy wheels, stereo upgrades, a rear spoiler, deck rack, polished treadplates, and so on.

American magazines regularly feature the Miata Mania Accessories Catalog, "jam packed with products designed to improve and personalize your car." Run down the classified ads, and you'll find Motorsport of California, Racing Beat (which was heavily involved in the success of the RX-7 in competition), Pacific Auto Accessories, Road Show International, and goodness knows how many others. Performance Techniques and Cartech International have both produced a turbocharger installation; Downing Atlanta and Nelson Superchargers of Los Angeles have gone down the supercharger route; and then there are the cars and accessories

TWR of England produced this RTM hard-top, and a novel aero cover. The latter came in two parts: a moulding around the seats and a cover that butted up to it. This cover could then be removed and stored in the boot, allowing the soft-top to be erected.

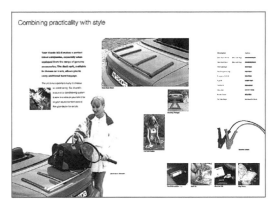

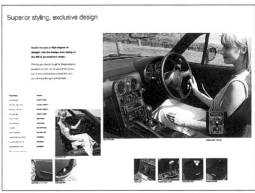

The Pit Crew Racing company of Suzuka offered this interesting conversion.

Pages from Mazda UK's official accessories catalogue of 1996.

Zoom Engineering of Tokyo produced this Lotus Elan lookalike.

Four pages from the Mazdaspeed brochure for the A-Spec aero kits. B-Spec modifications concentrated on the engine, with various states of tune being available.

produced by Rod Millen and Mazdasports. For something a little more adventurous, Performance Car Kraft of New Jersey offered Ford V8 conversion kits with uprated braking systems to suit.

In Germany, Samurai Tuning of Essen was quick to produce the Samurai MX-5. With subtle modifications to the lower coachwork, a nice faired-in hood cover, rear spoiler and 225/50 ZR16 tyres on wide alloy wheels, it was quite a tasteful package.

Mazdaspeed

Mazdaspeed, the factory's racing subsidiary, lists shock absorbers with four different settings, harder springs that also lower the car by 30mm (1.2in), thicker anti-roll bars and strut braces, plus harder shock mountings and lower arm bushes. It also stocks harder engine mountings, uprated brake pads for both front and rear, and uprated clutch components. Special exhaust systems, pistons, camshafts, lightened flywheels, an oil cooler, a modified gearchange, high performance air filters, and various viscous limited-slip differential units (plus a harder differential mounting rubber) round off the mechanical parts.

A number of engine tuning options are available, known as B-Spec modifications. Stage I takes a 1.6-litre engine to 130bhp, or a 1.8 to 145bhp. Stage II increases this to 144bhp on the 1.6, or 170 on the 1.8. There is also a supercharger kit, which boosts the 1.6 engine's power to 170bhp, and the 1.8-litre unit to 180bhp.

On the more cosmetic side, the list offers sportier sounding exhaust tailpipes, replacement dashboards, steering wheels, alloy wheels, gearknobs (with matching handbrake trim), various aerodynamic components, and a bucket seat. There's even a roll-over bar, which can also be specified with something Mazdaspeed calls an 'Aeroboard' – a device to cut buffeting in the cockpit.

For some time, Mazdaspeed has listed the A-Spec Aero Kit Type I and Type II alongside the B-Spec engine tuning menu, but, from April 1998, delivery of the Tokyo-based company's most adventurous project began: its first complete car for public sale. Known as the Roadster C-Spec, only 30 were ever built, but it was very significant nonetheless. Billed as "the final evolution," it featured some rather stunning coachwork modifications, plus a 200bhp two-litre Mazdaspeed Stage III engine. The basic version cost 4,350,000 yen, while the leather-trimmed Special was priced at 5,300,000 yen.

Modified packages in the USA

It's not surprising to learn that the Miata was soon the subject of a number of transformations in the States, some of which were done from a styling point of view, others from a performance angle. Occasionally, complete packages would be offered, a few of which are mentioned.

Rod Millen, the New Zealander who has done so much to promote Japanese cars through his exploits in motorsport (he's represented Mazda, Toyota and Nissan

Delivery of Mazdaspeed's first complete car for public consumption – the C-Spec – started in April 1998. Only 30 of these 200bhp machines were ever produced, but at 4,350,000 to 5,300,000 yen, they were mighty expensive. The leather-trimmed model cost about the same as the Nissan Skyline GT-R V Spec.

The Racing Beat body kit. So many bolt-on kits destroy the lines of the original vehicle, but one can still clearly see the distinctive MX-5 profile showing through on this restrained offering.

at top level), was quick to spot the potential in the Miata. Rod Millen Motorsport, operating from California, offered a turbocharged machine known as the Turbo MX-5 Miata.

As Richard Homan explained in a 1989 *Road & Track* special: "On the engine side of things, the team was able to draw heavily from its experience with a similar 1.6-litre dohc 16v fuel-injected powerplant of Mazda origin – that of the turbocharged 323 GTX, a longtime bread-and-butter Millen rally car ... Millen Motorsport raided the 323 GTX's engine, pirating the car's camshafts, pistons (thus lowering the Miata's compression ratio from 9.4:1 to 7.2:1), radiator, turbocharger and intercooler. The turbo implant is the golden nugget of the Millen Miata's performance upgrade. Tucked tightly into the engine bay, the little turbo is mounted stage left up against a Millen Motorsport-designed, stainless steel exhaust manifold ..."

Power was put in the region of 230bhp but, despite this, the standard gearbox was retained. A heavier clutch and a Millen limited-slip differential were used, however, as was an uprated suspension and braking package, the latter sourced from the RX-7 Turbo parts bin.

"Slung lower and filled out by the special 7J x 15 Rod Millen Motorsport directional aero wheels with 205/50 VR15 Bridgestone Potenza RE71R tyres, the Miata was beginning to look tougher; it was getting an attitude," noted Homan.

Thus, every aspect of the Miata's performance was improved. 0-60 was covered in 6.4 seconds instead of the standard car's 9.5, and the standing quarter was timed at 14.7 seconds (with a 95.5mph, or 153kph, terminal speed) – a full 2.3 seconds less. The top speed was now quoted as 126mph (202kph).

As for handling, the moderate understeer usually found in the stock Miata was reduced, helping the Millen car go through the slalom test quicker and pull 0.90g on the skidpan (against 0.83 for a showroom model). At the same time, braking distances were reduced to 85 per cent of those recorded with a standard car.

Of course, everything comes at a price, and, whereas the standard Miata cost $13,800, the fully loaded Millen car was roughly $25,600. This included the turbocharger ($650), intercooler and plumbing ($2200), modified camshafts ($300), pistons ($120), fuel management system ($1100), stainless exhaust manifold ($550), stainless exhaust system ($330), Centreforce clutch ($425), uprated brakes ($2240), limited-slip differential ($750), larger anti-roll bars ($350), spring set ($200), strut brace ($225), Panasport 7J x 15 alloys ($740), exhaust temperature gauge ($350), boost gauge ($32), Momo steering wheel ($210), rear spoiler ($195), and rear deck aero cover ($195).

The package was sold in Australia under the Racing Dynamics name. Yokohama 195/50 ZR15 tyres were

Japanese advertising for a number of American conversions.

fitted on Venette five-spoke alloys, but otherwise it was very similar to the car in the States. Some thought the price was a little high, but *Modern Motor* correctly pointed out that people happily paid a premium when the car was in short supply. The same Aussie magazine noted: "Improving on a design so widely commended was a difficult task, but the modified car does the trick."

Another company that transformed the standard Miata was Mazdasports of California, a newly established arm of Oscar Jackson Racing (of Honda fame), founded to exploit the potential of the Miata. Douglas Kott tried the car for *Road & Track* and was very impressed. He said: "The well-scuffed Yokohama A008Rs adhered to the 200 foot-diameter skidpad with a vengeance to generate 0.89g – 7 per cent more grip than the stock Miata on the same surface. At the cornering limit, its balance was commendable; a drop-throttle stunt that would have had the driver of the stock car cranking in lots of countersteer required only a minor steering correction in

the Mazdasports Miata to keep everything tidy and under control."

Racing Beat built a number of so-called 'California Miatas' to promote its aftermarket body panels. The full conversions included a new nose section, side skirts, a 'Streamline' rear deck cover, rear spoiler, and a restyled rear bumper.

Dave Hops of Monster Motorsports in California started modifying the Miata early in 1992. The 'Monster Miata' conversion basically involved swapping the four-cylinder Mazda engine for a 225bhp five-litre V8 from the Ford Mustang (complete with transmission), and then uprating suspension and braking components to suit. The brochure stated it was "Where the Far East meets the Wild West!"

Styling changes were amazingly subtle, resulting in the car looking like an M2 project, but performance freaks are usually more interested in figures: 0-60 in under five seconds was impressive enough to get the attention of

most people! More than 70 were built during the first four years, but, in the meantime, Hops introduced the 'Mega Monster.'

The Mega Monster, styled by Terry Choy, could be bought with a supercharged five-litre unit giving 400bhp, or a 5.6-litre lump producing an incredible 460bhp! Strangely, because the Mazda 1.8-litre four-cylinder engine is not particularly light, the Mega Monster conversion added only 120kg (264lb) to the weight of the car. Thus, even the 400bhp machine was capable of 0-60mph (96kph) in less than four seconds, and would happily go on to a claimed maximum of 160mph (256kph). Those not put off by its brute power would probably flinch at the $50,000 price tag. Not surprisingly, the Mega Monster is a fairly rare beast. However, Hops was also working on the Miata FXR – a turbo conversion boosting the 1.8-litre engine's output to a more reasonable 195bhp.

Another professional conversion was carried out by Dave Lemon of Mazdatrix, another Californian company more readily associated with the rotary engine. It therefore came as little surprise when Lemon – an ex-racing driver – used an RX-7 Turbo power unit to improve the performance of the Miata. With around 260bhp on tap, 0-60 came up in just 6.6 seconds, so the suspension and braking were suitably uprated to keep the car in check. The detailing was beautiful ...

In early 1995, *Car & Driver* carried an article on the PFS Miata SC. PFS stood for Peter Farrell Supercars, a Virginia-based company run by Farrell, an ex-racer who became heavily involved with Mazda's competition success in the States. Apart from selling the occasional 360bhp RX-7, Farrell also commissioned Craig Neff (who built rock group ZZ Top's famous Cad-zilla) to build the supercharged Miata SC. With 185 horses under the bonnet, the 0-60 time came down to 6.9 seconds, while the top speed was now around 130mph (208kph). Naturally, the suspension was uprated, and the Miata SC actually pulled a full 1.0g on a 300 foot skidpan. Production models were priced at $30,000.

Buying hints & tips

There's no doubt that the MX-5 has caught the imagination of the motoring public. In March 1996, *Auto Express* said: "This roadster is guaranteed to put a smile on your face. It looks great and provides the sort of driving pleasure few cars can match."

However, popularity like this always breeds plenty of opportunities for making money. While the vast majority of people dealing in the MX-5 and its aftermarket add-ons are as straight as the day is long, the same journal highlighted a new problem that every potential buyer should be aware of – secondhand cars imported from Japan which have either been damaged, or are no longer able to pass the strict tests carried out in that country after a car reaches its third birthday.

In mid-1997, *Auto Express* found that a large number of cars were coming into Britain with service histories in Japanese, and several had previously been involved in accidents. The engine management systems are different, and all home market vehicles are fitted with kph speedometers, giving an ideal opportunity to alter the mileage once it is replaced with an mph speedo. More recently, it has been uncovered that many of the cars stolen in Japan end up in Britain. Buyer beware!

Despite the flood of 'grey imports,' the MX-5 will hold its value pretty well, regardless of whether or not it's a limited edition model. In fact, Mazda UK issued a press release which referred to an in-depth study to find the lowest depreciating cars in the UK carried out by *What Car?* magazine. The release read as follows: "The *What Car?* survey, in the July 1991 issue, was conducted to advise its readers which new cars would suffer from the smallest amount of depreciation within the first 12 months of ownership. A total of 20 vehicles were assessed, with the Mazda marque taking three places.

"The Mazda MX-5, currently *What Car?* magazine's 'Sports Car of the Year,' was judged overall winner with the judges commenting: 'It's appealing on the road for all the right reasons – steering accuracy, delightful gearchange quality, great handling ability and carefree wind-in-the-hair motoring.' The *What Car?* panel determined that the Mazda MX-5 would depreciate by just 15 per cent in the first 12 months."

Placed in the under £17,500 category, the MX-5 was followed home by Toyota's MR2 (17 per cent) and the BMW 318i at 20 per cent; the Hiroshima machine received the *What Car?* award again in 1997.

The moral of the story is there's rarely a true bargain. If an MX-5 is cheap, be careful. On the other hand, don't pay too much for a car that's not worth it. Ask plenty of questions, insist on seeing its service history, and have the car inspected by a professional body. If the car has been modified, make sure it has been done properly.

Running an MX-5

The best advice one can offer here is join an owners' club. Unlike most car clubs, which only come into being once a model attains 'classic' status (usually based on age, examples becoming scarcer and parts more difficult to source), the MX-5 had organisations popping up all over the world the minute it was launched. In America, Norman Garrett (who, as you will have learnt from reading the earlier sections of the book, was heavily involved with the car while he was with MANA), founded the Miata Club of America. By the end of 1989, it was estimated to have almost 5000 members, and today that figure hovers around the 25,000 mark. With Chapters (branches) all over the country, the combined experiences of the membership will mean that someone, somewhere will have had a similar problem and, more importantly, found

With the right budget, one call to the right people at the factory, and you can now have what amounts to a brand new NA-type MX-5 off the peg ...

a way of overcoming it. There is even a UK Chapter (the MX-5 Owners' Club); Paul Grogan, ex-Chairman and co-founder of the club, kindly helped with some of the information for this book.

In Japan, as one would expect, there are numerous clubs. The biggest was founded by ex-M2 project man, Masanori Mizuochi, who is now the affable Chairman of the Roadster Club of Japan. The RCOJ came about in 1996 when a large number of smaller organisations decided to group together.

Rod Grainger of Veloce Publishing wrote and produced the *Mazda MX-5 Enthusiast's Workshop Manual* (known in America as the *Miata Enthusiast's Shop Manual*) to help owners complete DIY jobs on their car. It is probably the most useful investment an owner can make; there's helpful advice on every aspect of ownership. There is a manual for the original 1.6-litre models, and a separate one for the newer 1.8-litre cars.

The MX-5 is not a complicated car to work on, and keeping one on the road just got an awful lot easier thanks to the factory reissuing a number of consumables and other spares. Indeed, there is even a full rebuild service available for the NA, with the company renovating cars in much the same way as Nissan did with the 240Z at one time.

Mazda first offered rebuilt cars through a so-called 'Refresh Vehicle' programme, announced on 11 January 2003 to coincide with the Tokyo Auto Salon of that year. These were old shells, brought back to life by the Mazda E&T subsidiary, and all 30 cars on offer (five Version 1s, and 25 Version 2s) were sold by July. The new service is rather different, though, being more like the one punted

by Honda for the NSX in that it's aimed purely at existing owners – a restoration of their own car, rather than an opportunity created for those that missed out on the NA the first time around.

Officially announced in August 2017, the latest service covered a full body restoration with the TÜV-certified Mazda E&T outfit in Hiroshima fitting a whole host of new panels in the process before a full bare metal respray. Other options included an interior restoration, an engine and powertrain overhaul, a chassis and suspension rebuild, an air conditioning system rebuild, and a fresh alloy wheel and tyre package. Assuming the vehicle was in a suitable state to start with, owners could choose how far they wanted to go, for ticking all the options could add up to a minimum of 4,850,000 yen! Nonetheless, at the time of writing, three or four cars a year were going through the programme.

The beauty of this restoration service is that it has encouraged Mazda to reproduce an awful lot of components that will allow people to keep their cars on the road in 'original' trim. Mazda even asked Bridgestone to make new tyres in keeping with the early NA, and has had things like the first hood with a zip-in window and OEM-spec seven-spoke alloys remade. Amongst the 170 or so parts commissioned by the company are seatbelts, carpets, labels, and even the elegant Nardi steering wheel and gearknob seen on cars at the start of the 1990s. It should serve as an example for others to follow, for there are several well-known European makers who are letting down enthusiasts (the author included) through a lack of even the most basic spares for middle-aged machinery.

APPENDIX 2

NA-series production figures

The figures below are taken from official Mazda records. The table shows production figures and the number of cars exported in each year; running totals for both have been added in. Given the short production life of the model, the state of the world economy at the time, and sports car sales in general, these figures are very impressive.

Year	Production	Cumulative totals	Exports	Cumulative exports
1988	12	12	0	0
1989	45,266	45,278	34,021	34,021
1990	95,640	140,918	67,400	101,421
1991	63,434	204,352	40,729	142,150
1992	52,712	257,064	34,096	176,246
1993	44,743	301,807	27,909	204,155
1994	39,623	341,430	29,079	233,234
1995	31,886	373,316	27,648	260,882
1996	33,610	406,926	29,231	290,113
1997	24,580	431,506	22,856	312,969

Total number of NA series models produced   **431,506 units**
Total number of NA series models exported   **312,969 units**

This second table breaks down sales in the main markets, including, Japan, the USA, Canada, Europe (which includes the UK) and Australia.

Year	Japanese Sales	American Sales	Canadian Sales	European Sales	Australian Sales
1989	9307	23,052	2827	0	621
1990	25,226	35,944	3906	9267	1446
1991	22,594	31,240	2956	14,050	746
1992	18,657	24,964	2277	6631	502
1993	16,789	21,588	1501	4824	453
1994	10,830	21,400	1173	5019	404
1995	7178	20,174	934	7716	196
1996	4413	18,408	558	9585	241
1997	3537	17,218	594	10,480	206
1998	6	1376	NA	NA	NA
Totals	**118,537**	**215,364**	**16,726**	**67,572**	**4815**

Note: The 1998 figures for Canada, Europe, and Australia cannot be broken down at this stage, so the totals reflect those of 1997 for these particular markets.

The **Essential** Buyer's Guide

MAZDA
MX-5 MIATA
Mk1 1989-97 & Mk2 1998-2001

Your marque expert: Carla Crook

Having this book in your pocket is just like having a marque expert by your side. Benefit from the author's years of real ownership experience, learn how to spot a bad car quickly, and how to assess a promising one like a true professional. Get the right car at the right price!

ISBN: 978-1-845842-31-4
Paperback
19.5x13.9cm
64 pages
107 colour pictures

For more info on Veloce titles, visit our website at www.veloce.co.uk
email: info@veloce.co.uk
Tel: +44(0)1305 260068

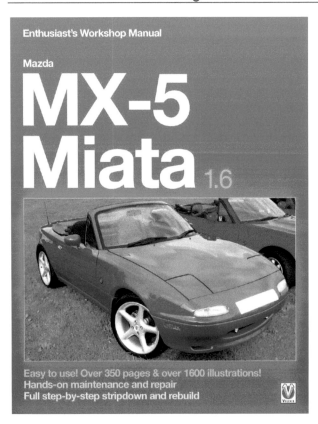

Friendly & easy to understand. Covers all 1989-1994 1.6 models, inc. Eunos. Rod stripped down an MX-5 in a domestic garage using ordinary tools & took over 1500 step-by-step photos. Details every aspect of important jobs.

ISBN: 978-1-787111-74-5
Paperback
27x21cm
368 pages
1600 pictures

For more info on Veloce titles, visit our website at
www.veloce.co.uk
email: info@veloce.co.uk
Tel: +44(0)1305 260068

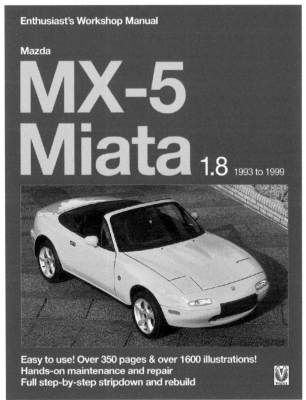

All 1.8 models, inc. Eunos, from 1994 (all pop-up headlight models). Phenomenally detailed, informative, helpful & easy to understand. Every detail of important repair & maintenance jobs is covered.

ISBN: 978-1-787114-20-3
Paperback
27x21cm
368 pages
Over 1600 illustrations

For more info on Veloce titles, visit our website at
www.veloce.co.uk
email: info@veloce.co.uk
Tel: +44(0)1305 260068

ISBN: 978-1-845843-88-5

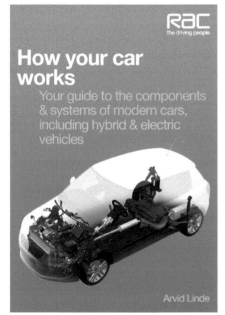

ISBN: 978-1-845843-90-8

ISBN: 978-1-845845-18-6

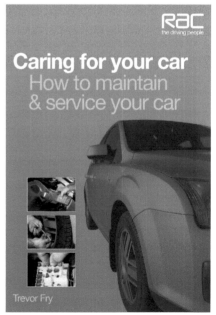

ISBN: 978-1-845843-96-0

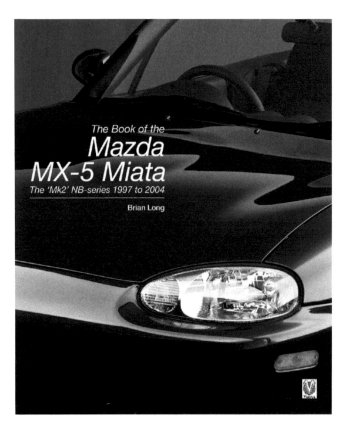

The definitive history of the second generation Mazda MX-5, which was also known as the Miata or the Roadster. The book focuses on the NB-series – covering all major markets of the world, and using stunning contemporary photography.

ISBN: 978-1-787111-93-6
Hardback
25x20.7cm
44 pages
290 pictures

For more info on Veloce titles, visit our website at www.veloce.co.uk
email: info@veloce.co.uk
Tel: +44(0)1305 260068

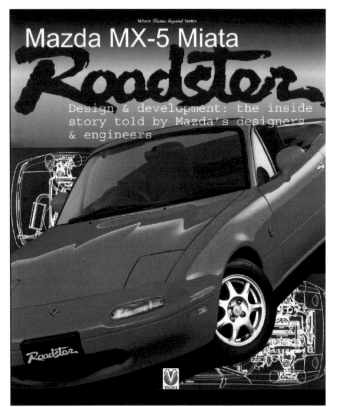

This is the fascinating inside story of the design and build of what would become the world's favourite lightweight sports car. Candid text, written by the engineers and designers themselves, guides the reader through every stage of the vehicle's development, from original concept through to the production model that took the world by storm.

ISBN: 978-1-787113-28-2
Paperback
25x20.7cm
176 pages
302 pictures

For more info on Veloce titles, visit our website at www.veloce.co.uk
email: info@veloce.co.uk
Tel: +44(0)1305 260068

INDEX

The Mazda company and its products are mentioned throughout this book.